The **Why:**

If public opinion polls for 2024 can be believed 65% of Americans are worried about the fate of democracy in America.

The author told the Library of Congress *this* regarding the **What:**

This book is intended to persuade voters to support the 2024 candidacy of the author, Harry Robb Welty, for Congress. It is a series of about 70 previously published anecdotes and personal reminiscences that suggest the dire changes that have taken place in the Republican Party to obliterate its origin as "the Party of Lincoln." The author, Mr. Welty, aims to bring Abraham Lincoln's spirit back into the Republican Party of today, 2024.

Cover photo by Andy Welty

NOT YOUR USUAL REPUBLICAN

Published by: Welty Press
2101 E 4th St.
Duluth, MN 55812 USA

Not Your Usual Republican
Subtitle:
Pro Trump = Anti-Lincoln

Harry Welty is a Republican who predicted Donald Trump would be the future of the Republican Party at Minnesota's 8th Congressional District Republican nominating Convention in 1992 which resulted in a loud chorus of Boos.
Volume One

ISBN #978-0-9632953-2-3
Library of Congress Control Number: 2024908511
First printing of Not Your Usual Republican - May, 2024
Printed in Duluth, Minnesota, United States of America

Dedication

Many thanks to loyal Democrat Patty McNulty who, along with Republican Bill Ulland, took me under their wings after I'd lost three Duluth School Board elections in 1989, 1991, and 1993. They ordered me to shut up while they got me elected. My daughter told them at the election night party that for once she wouldn't have to go to school wearing a paper bag over her head. Patty also suggested that the publisher of the Northland (now the Duluth) Reader publish a story I wrote about fighting army worms. Since then, I've contributed over 300 additional columns, a number of which are reprinted here. Others can be viewed online at duluthreader.com and snowbizz.com.

HARRY WELTY

Not your usual Republican

The Gretta Thunberg of the Republican Party, Harry likes Democrats. It's the American way.

Harry is a Snow sculptor, writer, and long time Duluth school board member

Campaigns at: www.weltyforcongress.com (where you can donate online)

Blogs at: www.lincolndemocrat.com

Podcasts at: Spotify, Not your usual Republican

Paid for by: Welty for Congress , PO Box 3181 Duluth, MN 55803

These are the front and back sides of Harry Welty's 2022 campaign card. Harry's not changing it for 2024.

NOT YOUR USUAL REPUBLICAN
TABLE OF CONTENTS

With one exception columns contained herein were written by Harry Welty and touch on his experiences and opinions.

The contents of this book are provided to give insight into a candidate for Congress who will confound his new colleagues with his generosity of spirit and take-no-prisoners candor. Written over a period of 23 years - some anecdotes will repeat in these columns.

FOUR INTRODUCTIONS

In no particular order, I will offer four introductions to this book. The book's purpose is to help me, a five-time candidate for Minnesota's 8th Congressional District seat, remove a Trump dittohead from Congress.

One intro is my speculation about what Lincoln's Army would have done as it marched through Washington, DC, after winning the Civil War if it had seen Trumpers attacking our Capitol like they did on January Sixth, 2021.

One intro reintroduces a fable that I wrote 22 years ago. My version turns the Emperor's New Clothes on its head into a nightmare.

One intro introduces my grandfather, George Seanor Robb. It's meant to remind us of the greatness the MAGA movement was invented to undo.

Finally, one intro is my reply to an email I received from Congressman Stauber, a "Trump dittohead," who has let Trump do all his thinking for him.

Introduction ONE

A day of treason revisited a year later
Thursday Jan. 13th, 2022

The Grand March through Washington after the Civil War, which began when traitors attacked Fort Sumter on April 12, 1861. Photo by Matthew Brady in the National Archives.

Here's a thought experiment: Imagine that the federal troops who entered the nation's Capitol in the "Grand March" after winning the   Civil War were suddenly transported to the nation's capital 156 years in the future to Jan. 6, 2021. As they proudly marched past, imagine what would happen if they saw people in strange modern dress waving Confederate flags battling to enter the nation's Capitol. What would these well-armed soldiers do?

I watched that invasion slack-jawed on television one year ago. Google: Duluth Reader, "Purging the RINOs" Jan 14, 2021. I have alternately seethed at what they did then and still are still attempting to do and my better angels. They were Lincoln's better angels before his brains were blown out by an early version of a Trump supporter.

I took heart in the wake of the spectacle. Some shocked Republicans condemned the attack, confident that the crime would be obvious to everyone. But cultists cannot see the obvious. Today, only a dozen congressional Republicans still have a shred of backbone. Lynn Cheney, an exception, has testicles enough for anyone of her spineless colleagues should they find the courage to sew a pair back on.

I would like to put the blame for this cultish behavior on the egocentric loser who has holed up in Mar-a-Lago, scamming his Grateful Deadish fans for money to pay his mounting legal bills. However, I just can't make myself follow the amiable example of Will Rogers who said: "I never met a man I didn't like." Trump loyalists are too historically ignorant to understand the legacy they champion springs from the South's defeat in the Civil War.

The losers rebuilt the South with a chip on their shoulder. They re-established their power and continued to turn their back on our founding document's founding principle that: "All men are created equal." It interfered with a state's right to deny some citizens their right to vote.

I personally rejoiced when three white Georgia men were recently sentenced to life in prison for chasing a black jogger down and shooting him like a dog or Abe Lincoln. When Sirhan Sirhan was given a life sentence for assassinating Robert Kennedy, I was gratified. I wanted him to spend the rest of his days in prison, not get off quickly with the death penalty. I am glad his recent paroles have been denied. He tried to kill America; just as slave masters once tried to kill America; just as Donald Trump is trying to kill America.

Although he'd bragged for 30 years that he would be a great President, it took being mocked by Barack Obama in 2011 to light a fire under him. It set him on a merry chase to rip the Republican Party's empty-suited, presidential wannabes into confetti as he seized the party's nomination for President.

You can see the moment the fire was lit somewhere on YouTube. President Barack Obama humiliated Trump in front of all the people whose respect the property developer craved. At a Press Club Roast, Obama twisted the knife into Trump for touring America claiming to have proof that the President, the son of one of my fellow Kansans, was a foreigner.

Trump would do Obama one better. He would get elected President. To do it, Trump racked up the most prodigious record of provable lies in Earth's history. His latest and biggest lie fueled his attempted coup.

No one likes to be made fun of. Many of Trump's supporters feel that people look down on them, too. Trump has done his best to reinforce this feeling. The year following the collapse of the coup has only made this all the more painful for them. They have watched a parade of wannabes groveling at Mar-a-Lago for the Pope's blessing. There has not been a single profile in courage among them.

But the bleeding-heart LIBERAL Republican in me can't help but feel sorry for these gullible people whose star is still milking them to pay for his legal bills. He's so busy he has abandoned those who heeded his call to ransack the Capitol to their prison sentences.

That said, ignorance has never been an excuse for a capital crime. Fortunately, America is a land that believes that no one is above the law, including a President.

The soldiers parading through our nation's Capitol 156 years ago in the Grand March were convinced that they had closed a terrible chapter of our nation's history. Donald Trump has done his best to keep it propped open. It's time we closed that book for good.

Everything Harry writes that is not about the imminent destruction of Earth as we knew it is superfluous. But, he does prattle on at lincolndemocrat.com.

Power Trip Dementia

Thursday Jun. 13th, 2019

      Dementia is a little like the intoxication of all-knowing youth. "Look, Mom, no hands," or "I know all about sex... Oops!" or maybe, "I can pay off my student loans once I have my degree."

      But only one American is made of financial Teflon. Donald Trump has repeatedly bullied and conned a major bank into lending him millions that he failed to repay. Then he sued them! The question for America is, are we as stupid as Deutsche Bank?

      While goody-two-shoes are appalled at Donald Trump's supporters, there is real genius behind the high school grads and blue-collar workers who elected him President. Unlike our disappointing political parties, it was obvious that Trump would shake things up. In Trump's case, it's because of his unique brand of dementia—one that blinds him to his mistakes and makes apologies unthinkable.

Surely, the Wharton School of Finance taught him that high tariffs only deepened the Great Depression and made it last a decade. But Donald Trump, sporting a Gorgeous George fright wig, wades through his swamp like Moses parting the alligators. He has cowed the grifting heirs to the party of Lincoln who have despoiled Abe's legacy while hiding behind the banner of fetus-hood. Many of the folks who elected him recognize him for what he is—a glorious fraud. They need to break off eye contact with his tweets or they'll have only themselves to shame come 2020 for their second mistake. I'm counting on Abe Lincoln's counsel here: "You can fool some of the people all of the time, and all of the people some of the time, but you cannot fool all of the people all of the time."

Let's hope that the fable I penned for the Reader 17 years ago doesn't come to pass.

The King is Naked
Published May 31, 2002

The King visibly stiffened at the sound of the small piping voice. The King's guards faltered at their reins and their horses reared causing the great palanquin to halt momentarily before lurching ahead. The King pitched forward in a most undignified manner. Only a quick step saved him from toppling over. The King did not turn back to look at the boy who had dared lift the blissful veil of ignorance.

The delighted boy beamed as faces all about him in the crowd turned toward him in acknowledgment of his discovery. The sudden and unexpected silence was broken by the King's shrill command to his horsemen to better control their mounts. The palanquin lurched forward again as the King's procession creaked magisterially down the royal thoroughfare.

The boy felt his father's grip tighten around his spindly ankles. He winced as he looked down. Although the temperature was mild his father's bald spot flushed an angry red. He leaned down uncertainly to his father's ear and reasserted, "The King is naked." Then to make sure his father understood he added, "Isn't he?"

The father said nothing but tightened his grip still more.

Before the King had disappeared from view a halo formed around the boy and his father as the crowd drew away from them. The spectators began fleeing to their homes and livelihoods. Some faces in the throng turned furtively to stare at them both, father and son. The sound of feet shuffling over dry pavement was joined with that of suppressed whispers.

The father turned on his heels too and tried to rejoin the crowd. Again, the boy implored, "The King was naked wasn't he?"

"Quiet lad," said the father in a curt and unfamiliar voice as he turned into his home bolting the door behind him and setting the boy on the floor. A passerby peered nervously through their window as he sped past.

"Boy," said the father. "You saw nothing. Do you understand me?"

"But why?" asked the confused and injured boy.

"Never you mind why," said his father with finality. "Don't let me or anyone else ever catch you saying that again. Do you understand me?"

The boy looked up at his father uncomprehending.

"Do you understand me?" His father repeated with genuine menace in his voice.

"Yes," the boy lied, too shocked to argue.

"Good," said the father. "Forget what you said at the parade today and maybe no harm will come of it."

But harm did come.

No customers visited his father's shop for the rest of the day. It wasn't until the next morning that a single customer came round. He hung back at the doorway and would not enter. Instead he glanced fearfully out into the street.

"I've come to collect my order," he sniveled. "It'll be

my last. From now on I'll do my business with the tanner at St. Crispin's Parish."

"What!" the father started. "But that's a full day's travel from here!"

"Don't think I don't know it!" said the figure in the doorway, "The King's guard have been making inquiries. About you…" he said, "… and your boy."

The visitor turned and peered anxiously down the street again. "Never mind my order," he quailed. Backing away the customer beat a hasty retreat. The boy rushed to the door and saw the man scurrying away from a troop of the king's guard, which was marching grimly toward the tanner's shop.

In the days that followed neighbors guiltily avoided walking past the tanner's empty abode. No proclamation was necessary.

The nation understood. No one in the land was more splendidly attired than the king.

Keep your fingers crossed that Trump's out of office before Antarctica melts or before vaccines lose their potency or before China infects all our cell phones with facial recognition tech. For more of Harry check out: Lincolndemocrat.com

The George Robb exhibit in the Kansas State History Museum in Topeka with his helmet ventilated from front to back. He used to hang it in his garage on High Street.

Death of a War Hero Pt. 6 - My 1972
Published Duluth Reader, Thursday Feb. 29th, 2024

On a beautiful Sunday in May my grandfather, George Seanor Robb, died five days shy of his 85th birthday. The year before on that birthday Topeka's Daily Capital wrote about the Kansas hero and their reporter's visit to the Presbyterian Manor where he resided. The Presbyterians didn't salt his food but they let him smoke his pipe.

A handsome man in uniform he received dozens of marriage proposals as he lay recovering from his war injuries in a military hospital on his return at war's end. He was one of a hundred soldiers who had been written up in Life magazine.

The story glorified **General Pershing's 100 heroes.** Mail from young women inundated the 30-year-old convalescent with marriage proposals. My grandfather was flattered but would eventually marry the music teacher he had met in Iola, Kansas. Winona McLatchey had kept up a busy correspondence with her soldier while he was in France. The marriage took its sweet time but eventually my mother, their second child, would be born nine years later when her father was 40.

That late start to child rearing was one of the reasons why my grandfather never came down from the pedestal he was put on for me. He was just too old and reserved. He remained a busy State Auditor until just a year before my parents moved to Minnesota. Before he retired I could visit my dad in the office of the State Insurance Commission and my grandfather in the Auditor's office while passing the wall mural of John Brown reaping the whirlwind. It was painted when my Mother was a girl visiting her father the State Auditor. My Mother liked telling people that if she had been born a boy she would have been entitled to attend West Point as the child of man who had been awarded the Congressional Medal of Honor.

During childhood crises my Mom always told me, "Don't cry Harry your grandfather was shot." I'll never know if Mom cried the day she took the call of his passing. She stepped outside to be alone.

For my part I was very aware that I'd just walked in a peace march days earlier and that my grandfather might very well have disapproved. Vietnam was one more war my Grandfather could blame on Democrats but would he have approved of my marching against it once American soldiers were sent there to fight and die? He lived by the motto "My country right or wrong." So too had Robert E Lee when he gave the state of Virginia his first allegiance after he turned down Abe Lincoln's offer to command the Union armies. Life and war are complicated.

Every summer we would return to Topeka and I would spend an afternoon with my grandfather self consciously making conversation with a man steeped in history. He took umbrage when I told him my fifth grade teacher taught us that Ulysses S Grant was a butcher to his men while Robert E Lee took care of his rebel soldiers. I also suspected that Grandpa blamed my liberal Republican Dad for talking his daughter into voting for Lyndon Johnson for President instead of his hero Barry Goldwater. My folks weren't impressed to hear the GOP's Barry Goldwater hint that he might nuke North Vietnam.

After we moved to Mankato my Mother returned every other month to visit her father for a week. She returned to tell me about his experiences. In rushing this column along I've cut off 1600 words worth of stories. One thing my mother always insisted was that her father was a man of honor.

George Robb was proud that his father called himself a "black republican." He was proud that his family were good friends to their neighbor Larry Lapsley whose name is on the road signs that pass their old property. Mr. Lapsley is interred just yards from my grandfather in Salina's Gypsum Hill cemetery. Larry Lapsley was an escaped slave.

George Robb was a white officer to black men from Harlem. He suffered three wounds over two days of fighting leading them into battle. In later years he wrote speeches about their courage under fire.

When appointed State Auditor replacing a Democrat who died during his term of office George Robb ignored Governor Landon's instructions to fire all the office's Democrats. He told the governor they were good people. He did this even though not long before the Democratic President Franklin Roosevelt had replaced him as Salina's postmaster with a Democrat.

During the Second World War, which he also blamed on Democrats, he wrote a forceful letter to his Alma matter, Park College, when they didn't want to enroll a Japanese-American student in the college. The young man's brother was fighting Hitler in the American army.

And though it grieved him that Democrats controlled the Presidency for twenty straight years he told my mother that he liked the democratic president Harry Truman who joyfully gave Republicans hell.

Now its my turn to give Republicans, or rather frauds who call themselves Republicans, a little Hell. I'm doing it to honor my grandfather. He was a man who shook the hand of a man who shook the hand of Lincoln. Its time the Grand Old Party returned to being the **Party of Lincoln!**

Harry Welty is a Republican dammit and he blogs at: www.lincolndemocrat.com

Introduction FOUR

Nitpicking Pete Stauber's email

Thursday Sep. 8th, 2022

"Harry,
Joe Biden's hypocritical, flip-flopping message says it all.
And history doesn't lie:" Joe Biden on Oct. 6, 2020: 'Unity over Division'"

Really, Pete, this was a month before Biden was elected. And it was why he was elected. And let's be honest. Biden meant it. And what's more for two years he mostly stuck with the unity message. And what was Trump saying before he faced the voters?

Trump was asked if he'd step down if he lost. TRUMP DIDN'T ANSWER THIS QUESTION! Instead, he said he could only lose if the election was stolen. And guess what Trump said when he lost?

It's been two years of Keystone Cops trying to prove that Trump won a majority. There are people today who say Lyndon Johnson killed JFK. In 50 years there will still be people who say Trump won.

But even though President Biden held his fire for two years, you call what he said this week "hypocritical."

Joe Biden on Sept. 1, 2022: "Donald Trump and MAGA Republicans are a threat to the very soul of this country.

Talk about hypocrisy, you ought to look in a mirror. You've sworn an oath to God twice to protect our Constitution. So where were you hiding on Jan. 6 from zip ties, bear spray and confederate flag spears?

If you get called to meet your maker I'm sure she will remind you that history doesn't lie. Before Trump was out of office he invited 30,000 angry Americans to Washington DC and sent thousands of them to hang the Vice President. For two years Joe Biden held his tongue. But he is our President and there's another election in two months. If Donald Trump can call a club a diamond Joe Biden can call a spade a spade.

And those spades were and still are busy digging. Pete do you know about 4chan? Have you watched the trials of the Proud Boys or the would-be assassins of Michigan's Governor? How about the people who chanted that they wouldn't let the Jews replace them?

That's little black mustache talk, Pete. Do you really think these are "very fine" people?

When you ran out of things to say on your own you quoted a website:

"From Townhall: 'Despite Biden's lies, the true enemy of our Republic is the radical left and its progressive agenda that embraces Big Government, censorship and political violence. For them, the ends justify the means, and

they will stop at nothing to destroy this great country. We've seen the lengths they're willing to go against President Trump. What do you think they're willing to do to you? As Trump has always said, 'In reality, they're not after me, they're after you. I'm just in the way.'"

If you are going to send this out under your name I have a couple questions to ask you.

Let's start with "Biden's lies." Do you have a list of them? I don't remember any that go beyond a little politicking. What's a radical? Is progress radical? Do fighting global warming; encouraging police to be less trigger happy; building a social safety net for millions of homeless; cleaning ground water count as "radical?"

Is going to the voters to advocate for such things radical and if it is radical what's wrong with putting such issues to a vote and letting the majority win?

Is "Big Government" automatically wrong?" America needed 90% income taxation to fight Adolf Hitler. And how about following people into the bedroom or into doctor's offices?

That's big government but that's what your side is pushing for?

Not only is it big government, but I think its wrong-headed government to force a 9-year-old rape victim to stay pregnant until she can be given a Caesarean section because her birth canal is too small.

I agree that stealing elections justifies a Boston Tea Party and maybe guns. Certainly, The Ukraine stands out as an example of what a nation should do when their Democracy is under threat. If you think your side was innocent of election theft while the Biden side was guilty, you should say so publicly. It would certainly have helped Trump's case if any of his judicial appointees had agreed with him. Thank heavens for honest law enforcement.

One thing that doesn't make me feel safe is loud, threatening rhetoric. For 30 years I watched my Republican Party ratchet up rhetoric to a fever pitch. Twenty-five years ago a speaker told Republicans at a Duluth convention I attended that pro-choice people like me were worse "mass murderers" than Hitler, Stalin and Mao-Zedong combined.

Today Texas is offering bounties on people who drive pregnant mothers across the border of Texas to states where abortions are still legal. Spy networks are being set up reminiscent of the the Chinese communists who sniffed out pregnant women to force them to have abortions to control their population.

Imitation is the sincerest form of flattery. Don't flatter yourself, Pete!

Harry Welty also runs his mouth off at lincolndemocrat.com.

PRIMARYING PETE

You need look no further than the back cover of this book to see why Peter Stauber needs to be primaried. He lied to God. He lied to America. He undermined the government of the people, by the people, and for the people. He has done it three times. He showed a few minutes of courage like he did when he almost got his head shot off by a disturbed man as a police officer. But his initial shock at the attempted coup against Congress gave way to wholehearted support for Donald Trump and the men with zip ties, nooses, and Confederate flags.

Then he compounded his cowardice by voting in lockstep with the Trump hive to throw out the legitimate votes of Americans who had just voted for a change in the nation's highest office. Mr. Stauber's first loyalty is to the man who betrayed our founding fathers and our democratic way of life.

I have a few more questions for Mr. Stauber.

1. Should gays go back into the closet?

2. Should we arrest obstetricians who preform In-vitro fertilization?

3. Does your way of life include grabbing pussies?

4. Is an elected official who knows Trump lost in 2020 but won't admit it worthy to be a Congressman?

5. Is being an independent thinker in the GOP like being an independent thinker in Putin's Russia?

6. Was Ronald Reagan's 11th Commandment **"Thou shalt not speak ill of a fellow Republican"** wrong?

7. When Trump called John McCain "a loser" were you cool with that? How about your wife the retired Commander. How did she feel?

How the Minnesota primary works.

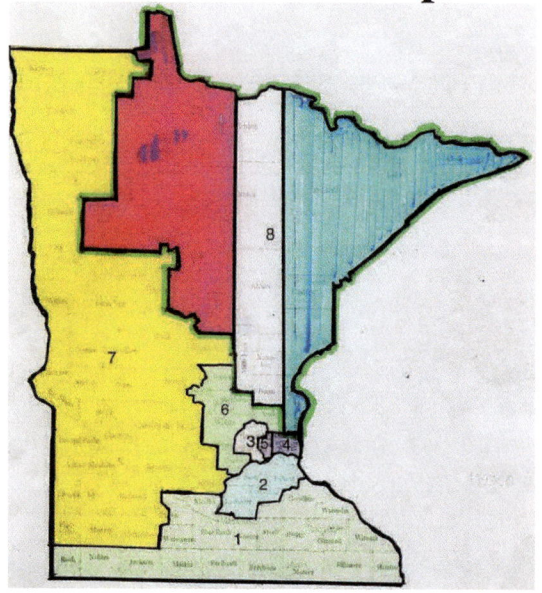

Minnesota's 8th Congressional Distict in Red White and Blue

Minnesota's largest congressional District #8 is shown in this map divided into 3 sections. Republicans (red) account for 40% of the voting population. Democrats (blue) account for 40%, and Independents (white) account for about 20%. Independents don't typically vote in primaries, although they have a right to do so in Minnesota. Here, every voter has a right to vote in the partisan primary of their choice for the five minutes it takes to select the best candidates for the general election.

The law was designed 100 years ago by legislators who did not trust political insiders. Any voter who admires President Lincoln is likely to be more of a Republican than anyone who supports Donald Trump. That's a lot more Republican votes than you will find among Trump supporters. Lincoln admirers should vote accordingly.

Without campaigning, Harry got 5% of the Republican vote in 2022. He will campaign this time. This book bears witness to that.

If Harry gets the lion's share of Independent votes, and if Democrats vote strategically on the Republican ballot and more Republicans join in to restore Lincoln's legacy, Harry would swamp Mr. Stauber in the primary. Democrats who want their candidate, Jen Schultz, to win in the general election would probably have an easier time defeating Harry than Pete. Not that I would make it easy for Jen.

I want Lincoln back in the GOP and in Congress. And I will vote for Jen if I do not become the Republican candidate. If you doubt that, look at the front cover of this book. I supported her in 2022 after I was defeated. In the 2020 primary, Pete got 39,000 votes. That was 10,000 votes fewer than Harry's 3,000 votes plus the 46,000 Democratic primary votes. If Democrats and Independents join with Republicans desperate for sanity, Pete would lose.

And what sweet justice. Primaries are how moderates were purged from the Party of Lincoln in the first place. Anyone familiar with how Europe bowed to Germany in 1939 should be able to follow the logic of this recent column.

Pete's way is Trump's way is the Dictator's way.

Duluth Reader, Feb. 17th, 2022

First they came for the socialists, and I did not speak out – because I was not a socialist.

Then they came for the trade unionists, and I did not speak out – because I was not a trade unionist.

Then they came for the Jews, and I did not speak out – because I was not a Jew.

Then they came for me – and there was no one left to speak for me.

–Pastor Martin Niemöler

Congressman Pete Stauber wrote recently under the hashtag: #OurWayofLife, "Together, let's defend our way of life, take back our country, and rebuild our future."

Whose way of life Pete? The trade unionists, the socialists, the Jews? How about the voters?

Your President Trump, whose pocket lint you have been picking for five years, doesn't like it when the voters call the shots. Your Donald Trump is an interesting animal.

When an assortment of fascists marched through Charlottesville in 2017 carrying tiki torches and chanting "Jews will not replace us," how did our first President with Jewish grandchildren defend his little ones? He called the Jew baiters "good people."

I'm sure Pastor Niemöler was rolling in his grave.

Unlike Trump in 2021 I accepted his victory in 2017. I didn't move to Canada. My country had not been taken away from me. But after years of watching Pete's kind of Republicans fiddle with elections I wonder if Pete's way is a country that includes me.

Who else is unwelcome? Gays? Black Americans? Women? University grads? Teachers? Pacifists, Agnostics? At least there's room for tiki torch bearers.

As I write this Vladimir Putin's army and navy surround the nation of Ukraine that Trump leaned on to help him win the 2021 election. Poor Ukrainians. By next week Trump's hero may plunge the world into the costliest war since my Dad went off to fight in 1943.

Throughout his presidency Stauber's man Trump showed deference to a succession of the world's most corrupt dictators and strongmen like North Korea's Kim Jong-un, Brasil's Bolsonaro, Philippine president Duterte, "China's" Xi, but above all Trump groveled at Vladimir Putin's feet.

The British writer Lord Acton's warned us long ago that, "power corrupts and absolute power corrupts absolutely."

These men all fit that description and Donald Trump is not far behind. I have probably missed 40 to 60 mail deliveries since Trump appointed Louis DeJoy as our nation's 75th U.S. postmaster general.

Evidently the President wanted to make sure absentee ballots weren't delivered to election officials in time to be counted. The man's a genius.

As a kid I thought the glory days of such tyrants like Hitler, Mussolini, Tojo and finally Stalin were a thing of the past. Then we elected an unscrupulous narcissist incapable of telling the truth who wanted to get in on the act.

Trump world has kicked American corruption to a level not seen since the Gilded Age between the Civil War and Teddy Roosevelt 1860-1900.

Until his election I wouldn't have guessed that Pete Stauber would willingly be an enabler to such a man. Pete's only infamy up to his election was getting the smallest college hockey team in history the biggest prize in college hockey – a 1988 Division One championship by not getting caught cheating.

Wikipedia quotes a sport's reporter as saying what Pete did was: "risky, arguably crafty, and in-arguably illegal."

Cheating, like drugs, starts small. First its lifting your own goal post off its pins when the ref isn't looking, then its stealing an election. Pete's team visited the Reagan White House which Pete said set him on the path to Congress. He must have missed it when Ron told the Rooskies to "tear down this wall!"

So, what are the ways of Pete's kind of people?

He hasn't said boo about the Jan. 6 crowd who tore down the blockades in front of the nation's Capitol and beat his fellow police while boasting of their plans to lynch Vice President Pence.

They are in hiding now disguised as anti-maskers blocking North American highways to cripple Biden's, and our nation's, economy. They are like BLM and anti-Vietnam war protesters only they've been strangling the economy for a week.

That's not my way of life. Whose is it? Hitler's people gave us Kristallnacht and burned down the Reichstag giving Adolph the Chancellorship in 1933. That was Hitler's way.

The Ukraine is Putin's way. Uighur genocide is Xi's way. Extrajudicial murders of methamphetamine addicts is Duterte's way. Burning the Amazon for leather SUV seat covers is Bolsonaro's way.

What is Pete Stauber's way?

If Pete Stauber fit into a set of Matryoshka dolls he would be the littlest. Me too, only my set would include General Dwight David Eisenhower, Teddy Roosevelt and Lincoln.

Everything Harry writes that is not about the imminent destruction of Earth as we knew it is superfluous. But, he does prattle on at: lincolndemocrat.com.

TORNADO ALLEY

I was born 20 days before the beginning of the second half of the twentieth century on December 10th, 1950. I was the first grandchild for both the widowed Ruth Welty and George and Winona Robb. We resided in Topeka, Kansas, smack dab in the middle of the lower 48 states whose stars then flew on the American flag. I come from good stock, and my stock told family stories.

Except for the first anecdote, these are my versions. The stories have added up as the generations traveled along tornado alley from the once bloody Kansas-Missouri border to Minnesota. The first anecdote is a short reminiscence from my father's youngest sibling, Mary Welty Hutchison. Her father Henry Harrison Welty only met my Mother once or twice before he died of a heart attack on a sales call at the age 49 before my parents' marriage. Henry Harrison Welty was known to all as Harry. I am a Harry (on my birth certificate), not a Henry.

Dribbles
Mary Welty Hutchison

There were two items in my house which were not what they seemed. The first was a can marked "Delicious Peanut Brittle" which actually held three tightly coiled, cloth covered springs, and the second was a delicately etched, normal looking goblet with tiny holes concealed near the rim, a dribble glass.

Although it was my father who had purchased these practical jokes to pull on his own children, my brothers and I quickly took delight in making victims of all visitors to our house.

"Care for some peanut brittle?" one of us would offer, passing the untruthful can to a guest. "The lid sticks a little," we explained as our victim wrenched opened the can. Flying cloth springs popped into the unsuspecting face, causing a quick intake of breath, a look of terror and an involuntary jump backwards, in that order. Dan, Frank and I, eagerly waiting for this moment, considered the outcome unbearably funny. With my grade school pals, Franks's high school buddies and Dan's college fraternity brothers, it was a great hit.

The dribble glass created a more subtle prank. The unsuspecting guest would not catch on for awhile, sipping most of the lemonade rushed out from the kitchen, wondering where those

wet spots were coming from. Perfect hosts, we kept the victim talking, eagerly intent on the conversation, watching every move of glass to lips, smiling broadly until the joke was discovered. Innocent fun. At least it was until the Reverend Dr. Orlo Choguill came to call.Katy Choguill, the Reverend's ten year old daughter, was at our house, playing, but Dr. Choguill probably didn't know that. At her tender age Katy was my encyclopedia of knowledge, not surprising with her brilliant father, but while he philosophied about that which is spiritual, Katy concentrated on the here and now. Slightly rebellious anyway, she loved practical jokes and had taken a fancy to our can of peanut brittle and the dribble glass, items which the Choguills were

unlikely to have in their home. I mention Katy, not to throw aspersions in her direction, but only because ever afterwards no one would claim responsibility for what happened to Dr. Choguill.

My father was a continual consternation to the good minister. Although dutifully giving

his money to the church and happily sending his wife and three children to listen to the sermons, he yet refused to go himself. Dr. Choguill took it as his personal goal to get my father inside the sanctuary, wanting him to hear the good news. Hence, the visit to our house.

The two men sat on the screened in front porch. My father, a chain smoker, held his customary cigarette in one hand.

This sin made him uncomfortable around the minister, feeling that Dr. Choguill probably disapproved of his smoking. In truth, smoking was the reason my father didn't go to church. He couldn't live for one hour without nicotine, such was his addiction.

Mother, fixing up a plate of cookies and a pitcher of lemonade, sent Katy and I out to the porch with a tray for the gentlemen. Unfortunately, that dribble glass was on the tray. Later, I swore I didn't put it there, but nobody believed me.

At first he didn't notice that anything was out of the ordinary, and then, in horror, my father realized that the lemonade had soaked Dr. Choguill's tie and was spattering onto his shirt and suit coat. He bit his lip, took a drag on his cigarette, and then, quite unexpectedly, burst out laughing.

Dr. Choguill took it pretty well, I thought, but he gave up on my father after that, and he never came calling again.

Uncle Frank's Smudge Pots
Not Eudora
Published April 1, 2004

I'm not in the mood. I know it's April First but I'm just not in the mood. Yesterday I visited Dealey Plaza in Dallas. After a couple of hours soaking up JFK's last moments I solemnly drove back to my motel over the same strip of pavement where Jackie tried to scramble out of her limo when a bullet burst through her husband's skull. And if that's not enough to darken a Texas sky I'm halfway through a book on another martyred President, Abraham Lincoln. Nope. I'm just not in the mood for April Fools.

Instead, I'll share some glass-half-empty tidbits about Uncle Frank. My Uncle Frank has no use for politics. When he visited us last summer he got hold of the column where I explained that I would be campaigning for reelection to the School Board as a "spineless bastard." He enjoyed that.

Uncle Frank is jaded about politics. His cynicism damn near cost the family the farm a couple years ago when he got aggravated with some county commissioners back in Kansas. I blame this disposition on Uncle Frank's lifelong subscription to the New Yorker. He wasn't always this way.

Frank began life a namesake to the "inalienable rights" of the Declaration of Independence. "Happy," for that is what his parents called him, was blissfully unaware of any other state of mind. He was a lucky child. My father, Frank's older brother Daniel, once looked on as a herd of horses broke free from a nearby slaughter house and thundered through the neighborhood. Happy was toddling along in the middle of street on his tricycle. Their mother was standing on the other side of the street. Two voices called simultaneously from opposite directions for Happy to run to them as a hundred hooves bore down on the boy. Happy stopped dead in his tracks and looked both ways unsure which direction to turn. A moment before impact the herd veered off leaving Happy unscathed. Ah, but too much grace can be a burden.

Much to his mother's dismay Uncle Frank continued to pursue his bliss. When detained after school for some infraction he simply crawled out the window and gamboled about on the school's roof while his acrophobic Mother looked on helplessly several floors below. Her natural instinct was to rein in her son's happy pursuits which she was inclined to blame on his friends rather than any property passed along through her family's bloodline.

There was, for instance, the time she walked into her house to find a passel of condoms strewn over the dining room table. "Stinky has done this!" she wailed, referring to one of Frank's aptly named buddies. But Frank protested that he was, in fact, the lucky discoverer of this treasure trove of balloons. He proudly told her how he had blown them up, tied them to his bicycle, and driven them all over the neighborhood. *All over!*

After one misadventure too many his Mother insisted that the family take Frank on a drive to the grounds of the state reform school. Here in the shadow of the valley of death Uncle Frank was shown where his carefree life would lead him. Somehow Uncle Frank survived this object lesson unchastened.

My Uncle took a special delight in tormenting his mechanically incompetent older brother. For instance, Dad was utterly helpless when his younger brother removed all the tires on his car during a date with my Mother. It was but a preview of coming attractions.

My Father was particularly deferential to my mother's father, Mr. Robb; a war hero turned Kansas State Auditor. First elected to the Auditor's post as a Republican in the early Thirties, George Robb had become a fixture in state politics facing only token opposition each election. One evening after a date with my mother, dad drove to her home only to discover that Frank had littered the Robb lawn with dozens of burning smudge pots (road construction warning signs from an earlier era) and dozens of lawn signs from Mr. Robb's hapless Democrat opponent. Mortified, my parents hid the garish spectacle before grandfather could discover it. Grandfather was quite amused when told of the prank.

Sadly, Uncle Frank had to grow up eventually and set "Happy" aside. He went away to war, returned home to study dentistry, then set up a dental practice in the foothills of the Rocky Mountains. He made the acquaintance of a Colorado legislator and loaned the villain a significant sum of money for a land deal which the law maker had an interest in. Alas, the loan was never repaid which taught my uncle a valuable lesson about the disreputable nature of politics and politicians.

29

Unfortunately, I can think of no useful moral to conclude this series of anecdotes with. I myself rather like politicians who have a bit of Uncle Frank in them or at least a little bit of his earlier incarnation, "Happy." I prefer to think that being a spineless bastard is an entirely curable condition the remedy for which is little more than a few smoking smudge pots. I'll bet Jack and Abe would both have agreed with me on this point.

Welty is a small time politician who lets it all hang out at: www.snowbizz.com

Gone with the Wind
Not Eudora
By Harry Welty
Published Aug. 1, 2008

As a little kid growing up in Topeka, Kansas, my family would often troop down to the basement when civil defense sirens warned us that conditions were ripe for tornadoes. I always wanted to stay above ground to see a twister like the one that blew Dorothy Gale's house onto the Wicked Witch of the East. When one did plow through a nearby farmstead or hamlet my dad would pack us into the car so we could gawk at uprooted trees.

Three years after my dad moved us to southern Minnesota, the far northern end of Tornado Alley, a finger of God ripped through seven miles of Topeka. It was two blocks wide at its worst and did extensive damage for a block on either side of that.

My grandmother survived because she and her daughter, my Aunt Mary, were visiting her step mother's apartment six blocks from her home. This apartment was in one of the block wide zones on either side of the main event. Aunt Mary refused to let her hop in her car and drive home after the sirens sounded. The three women bustled to the basement and listened as the freight train passed overhead.

In the stillness that followed my grandmother raced to her car to check on her home. It took her an hour to find a path free of fallen trees to reach it. It had blown off its foundation and was resting next to Eleventh Street. Her brick garage was gone.

I had just finished the ninth grade and was ruing my father's unwillingness to head immediately south to survey the damage. This left all the fun of the initial clean up to my uncles.

When we finally made it to Topeka, a week after the disaster, the devastation was still breathtaking. It was the costliest tornado disaster in US history up to that time, $100 million in 1966 dollars. The elm trees that hadn't already succumbed to Dutch Elm were limbless specters. I only had 12 exposures in my Yashica camera and had to husband them carefully on my long walk to Nana's. Everything I saw along the familiar route was worthy of a picture. My non gawking mission was to look for salvageable items especially silverware that Uncle Ned and Frank had missed.

I could look down into the corner of the basement where my grandmother dutifully hid when tornadoes threatened. Had she been there on June 8th she would have been buried by bricks flying loose from her garage. Had she survived this battering she might have drowned from the downpour that accompanied the wind. Had she survived this she might have been electrocuted by downed live wires that fell into the basement. Or, she could have been blown away like my Aunt Mary's little black dog which had been left in the sunroom. Its name wasn't Toto but it should have been. He found his way back to the house a few days later after a harrowing trip that my grandmother would have been unlikely to survive. Indeed, five or six residents of my grandmother's block were among the 17 killed by the tornado. Two more were killed in the bowling alley across the street when the billiard table they hid under crushed them.

The ceiling over Nana's front stairway was sky. The back stairs had been twisted so that descending them required me to step on the once vertical risers the treads having abandoned their horizontal position.

I spent an hour digging through the debris. I found one decorative porcelain plate that had somehow escaped chipping and a number of silver spoons. I carried these trophies back along with the dozen pictures I had taken. You can see the state capitol dome in one of them beyond Nana's house. It narrowly missed the fate of the 10 story National Reserve Life Insurance Building a little to its right.

My grandmother had opened my first savings account with a five dollar deposit in the Savings and Loan located in the National Reserve's first floor. The tower had also housed a barber shop where my father was getting a trim the time a man leapt to his death outside the plate glass window. The National Reserve tilted after the tornado hit it and had to be evacuated. The Company's motto was painted on the side of the building facing my grandmother's home: "A refuge in time of storm,"

The morning after, as other Topekans sifted through the debris of 800 destroyed and 3,000 damaged homes, my grandmother went looking for a place to stay. Her alacrity got her a nice apartment at a reasonable rent just before scarcity drove prices through the roof.

It's often said that progress follows disaster like light follows at the end of a storm. Today you can buy a happy meal at the McDonalds that took the place of my grandmother's home.

Welty is a small time politician who lets it all hang out at: www.lincolndemocrat.com

The monsters we need

Thursday Apr. 29th, 2021

Tragic Prelude, a mural completed by John Steuart Curry in 1937, now hangs in the State Capitol in Topeka, Kansas.

I was born in the cradle of the Republican Party – Kansas.

Despite my 55 years residence in mayonnaise Minnesota, I think my birthright gives me a better handle on today's Republican party than Canadian-born columnist David Brooks.

He's not wrong. In a dire NY Times column, Brooks tells of a January poll. It asked if politics is more about "enacting good public policy" or "ensuring the survival of the country as we know it."

Democrats answering the question chose policy but not Trump Republicans. They chose fear. Fifty-one percent of them said politics is about survival. And that doesn't mean global warming or surviving a pandemic.

That might have shocked our founding fathers, who wrote a Constitution to ensure a government that would act under the assumption that all men were created equal, since amended to include women and formerly enslaved men. We even fought a Civil War to make it thus.

That was then. Brooks quoted today's Trumpian Jack Kerwick who wrote, "The good man must spare not a moment to train, in both body and mind, to become the monster that he may need to become in order to slay the monsters that prey upon the vulnerable."

Really?

Does Mr. Kerwick mean that the American soldiers who landed on Omaha Beach and liberated Dachau were our equivalent of the Nazi SS?

Or a little closer to home?

Is Kerwick making a distinction between George Floyd and Derek Chauvin?

If so, I wonder which man would be which monster?

I fear the answer is black and white.

The Kansan in me wonders what Mr. Kerwick would make of John Brown, who killed a Kansas family in cold blood for supporting slavery and later went to the gallows after trying to start a slave revolt in Harper's Ferry, Virginia.

If Mr. Kerwick visited the Kansas State Capitol he would see how Republican Kansas honored Brown in the mural my mother saw painted during her visits to her father, George Robb, in the state Auditor's office.

John Steuart Curry painted John Brown reaping the Kansas whirlwind. While many state's lay claim to founding the Party of Lincoln, Bloody Kansas was the Civil War's first battlefield.

The Robb family's neighbor in Assaria, Kansas, Larry Lapsley, was a slave who escaped through rebel territory during the Civil War to reach freedom in Kansas.

At Lapsley's death, great grandfather Thomas Robb, a man proud to call himself a "black Republican," the equivalent of a "N----- lover," helped prepare his neighbor for burial. He returned home in a dark mood and ever after refused to talk about what he'd seen. My grandfather suspected that Larry had been castrated by his owners.

Castration, servitude, Jim Crow and mass incarceration have made some white Americans feel safer. This sorry history goes back before the 1830 slave revolt led by Nat Turner. After slaughtering slaves in revenge Virginia made teaching them how to read and write a crime.

But in Kansas the monster, John Brown, stands defiant under Topeka's capitol dome.

George Robb opposed America's sticking its nose in the wars of other nations. He had only voted for Democrat Woodrow Wilson because of his promise to keep American soldiers out of European trenches.

And yet he volunteered when war came and found himself leading black soldiers called the Harlem Hell-fighters. After the blood and dust settled my grandfather was awarded the Congressional Medal of Honor. With these laurels he was appointed to fill the vacant post of Kansas Auditor. He never again made the mistake of voting for a Democrat.

But as much as he opposed them he couldn't help but like Harry Truman. After fighting in the trenches he surely thought Truman's integration of the Armed Forces was long overdue.

Kansas put John Brown in the Capitol but the state was fainthearted about race. It segregated its elementary schools but not its high schools.

When she was sufficiently mature my mother sat side by side with black children. Even then Topeka High kept separate black and white sports teams, separate principals and stopped building a swimming pool in its basement when Topeka realized that children of all colors would swim in its waters.

Two years after my birth Kansan Dwight D. Eisenhower became president as a Republican. Ike's choice for Chief Justice of the Supreme Court, Earl Warren, fashioned a unanimous decision on the court's most tumultuous decision of the 20th century – Linda Brown vs. Topeka Board of Education.

From John Brown to Linda Brown, Kansas has led the nation.

Because of it I sat side by side with African American children in elementary school. I doubt that Derek Chauvin or Mr. Kerwick have ever had such an experience.

Officer Chauvin's suburb has but a 6 percent black population while his job was to over-police Minneapolis's black population, stopping people for petty offenses like being too poor to pay court fines or for failing to put on current license tabs in a timely fashion.

And what white cop who had never grown up with black kids wouldn't be nervous about policing black men half of whom had prison records in a nation awash with NRA protected guns.

It seems Derek Chauvin became the very monster Mr. Kerwick warns us we will need more of.

Harry Welty is a black Republican who charges at lincolndemocrat.com.

The gift of why

Thursday Apr. 9th, 2020

Charlotte Seanor Robb reading to granddaughters Mary Jane and Georganne in 1934

My mother told me that her beloved grandmother had a nightmare as she raised her four sons in the wilds of Kansas, just spittin' distance from where a tornado transported Dorothy Gale to the Land of Oz.

It wasn't the wild winds that frightened Charlotte Seanor Robb. It was the possibility that one of her boys might marry a "dirty" Swedish girl.

When I first heard this story, like my Mother, I thought it was humorous. I didn't think the Robbs could have been that much different than their Swedish neighbors. They all dug holes, "dugouts," into the banks above the Smokey Hill River to raise their families. They were all waiting for a propitious time to build a home on the flood plain. Thomas Robb finished his just before the birth of his sixth and last child, my grandfather.

When I moved to Minnesota, I learned that Swedes were clean living, sauna loving, civically minded people. Heck, even the addled Adolf Hitler thought Scandinavians were perfect representatives of his god-like "Aryan" race.

So, why did my mother's beloved grandmother take such a dim view of her neighbors? I have an answer now but it's not THE answer.

I have this opinion in large measure because my mother taught me through her example the gift of WHY. She loved having deep conversations with her friends and neighbors about the people they knew. I suppose it was gossip but, if so, the word has earned an undeserved reputation for mean-spiritedness.

Mom was simply doing what our ancestors did long before they took fully human form. They watched each other taking everyone's measure. It was a means of survival.

Which member of your group would pluck tasty pests from your back?

Which would share food?

Which would pummel your offspring if they were in a bad mood?

A few million years later this observant behavior made us what we are; the most social of animals, including some mighty insightful novelists.

Being observant might have offered her survival tips but for my Mother talking with and about her neighbors was simply an expression of her great desire to understand why. Why are we the way we are? Who isn't interested in that question?

Every time I write the stories my mother told me about family and friends the question of Why is foremost in my thoughts. As for the why in my great grandmother's anti-Swedish attitude I've given it a lot of thought.

A lot of white Americans (We're talkin' melanin deficiency here, not Aryan blood) are afraid they are about to be "replaced." That's what the alt-right, tiki torch bearers who ran over a liberal-minded girl in Charlottesville, Virginia, are afraid of.

The odd thing is that genetics proves that these marchers are an amalgam of peoples who in earlier generations regarded each other the way great grandma Robb regarded the dirty Swedes – as contaminated.

She was born into Pennsylvania in 1852 at the peak of the Know Nothing Party. Also known as the American Party, its members wanted to keep Germans and Irish out of America. The farthest back we've traced Charlotte Seanor's ancestors was to her grandfather, John George Zehner. He was born in Pennsylvania in 1794 or 95, twelve years after the Treaty of Paris ended the American Revolutionary War.

One result of the peace was a momentous decision by many Hessian soldiers who had been rented by King George to fight the Americans. Given a choice of a sea-sickening voyage home to get shot up in some new war or the temptation to settle in a lush and empty land they chose to stay.

John George's father was probably trying to kill General Washington during that war, but when the dust settled, pragmatic Pennsylvanians welcomed him to move next door. His labors would give them a customer for their goods and help make Pennsylvania prosperous.

Not that everyone was thrilled to have German-speaking neighbors. The Zehner's lost their German language and became the almost English sounding "Seanors." They shrugged off everything but sauerkraut, which the Robb boys helped their mother make five generations later.

Now thoroughly American, Grandma Robb couldn't help but fret about her Swedish neighbors even though they would follow her great-grandfather's example. At least that's what "the why" my mother taught me practice, leads me to believe.

Of course, the Americans bringing guns to the border to keep the Central Americans out have taken things a step or two farther than Charlotte Robb. My why tells me that they see the Indian gene pool, returning north to the U.S., the same way Charlotte saw her Swedes. But that's just my, why.

Not everyone likes a why. A lot of kids have learned to stop asking it. I'll be honest though. There are few things that unnerve me more than a head without a little why in it; especially with the promiscuous rights our Second Amendment bestows upon us.

Harry Welty wonders why at lincolndemocrat.com.

The Reverie of a Busy Mind at 4 AM, December 3, 2019

Thursday Dec. 5th, 2019

Charcoal sketch of Daniel Marsh Welty by his wife, Georganne, circa 1960

I woke up thinking about my dad, long gone these 33 years. A parade of thoughts, one after another strung together like the last thoughts of a man falling to his death. Dad, the 14-year-old who made lists of the candidates his parents should vote for in his indignation at the corruption of Democrat, Boss Pendergast in next door Kansas City. Who walked irradiated Hiroshima weeks after it was leveled. Whose younger brother removed his car's tires and left it on cinder blocks before his first date with my mom knowing that dad didn't know the difference between a hammer and a crescent wrench. The young man given a job in his Uncle's bank who along with the other impressionable young tellers were traumatized by the ribaldry of a coworker who regaled the boys with tales of her many abortions. This during the Eisenhower Era in Arkansas City, Kansas, four miles north of Oklahoma grown rich by defrauding Indians out of their oil. Who offered his public official boss the unwelcome advice not to accept expensive gifts from the companies their office was charged to regulate, and who wisely left to take a job working in Minnesota to teach and who taught well despite letting loose an infamous stream of profanity in class. Who tried to bribe me during my awkward stage by offering me fifty cents for every girl I cut the rug with. Who taught me to count to 100 and who helped me collect the stamps of nations he was eager to travel to. Who was a champion for the idea of hosting the first black student to enroll at my high school and who told me I would live to a ripe old age even as he secretly expected to die at age 49 like his father before him. Who told me of the power of self fulfilling prophecies and, in his last act, proved it by dying far too young and worse, went to his maker knowing that his son who kept losing local elections had just lost his third teaching job through sheer incompetence.

Maybe all these thoughts were prompted by my Father-in-law's death two days ago while the eighth snowiest blizzard in Duluth's history bore down on us. Maybe it was the hours of lonely snow shoveling the following day. Maybe it was the three shrews I saw racing with a will over the beautiful barrenness of fresh snow to hunt down half their body weight in prey by the end of the day. One hid in a hole my boot had made. Another caught my attention by cutting loose a string of shrewish expletives that would have made my dad smile. He was taking issue with a crow that took him for an easy meal but the shrew, no bigger than my thumb, lunged at the pterosaur and knocked it back on its tail feathers. Then it dashed for safety to the corner of my garage. Maybe he cast a jinx because two days later a city snowplow dislodged a decorative boulder that knocked bricks from the corner where the shrew had hidden.

After crawling out of bed to type up these stray thoughts I peered out the window by our annual Christmas jigsaw puzzle. Three stars shined through our city's light pollution. Even in the darkest unlit corners of Earth the naked eye can only distinguish a couple thousand stars, and these are our neighbors. If our bodies were the Milky Way these few stars would stretch no farther than across our fingernails. Missing from our eyesight are two hundred billion additional stars. At light speed it would take a photon forty 100-year lifetimes to reach the farthest of these visible stars. It would take 10,000 100-year lifetimes for it to reach the far side of the Milky Way. And beyond this lie a trillion other galaxies. I take some satisfaction in knowing that we humans are each of us a galaxy composed of a trillion symbionts and parasites living alongside our cells. It takes a special planet to keep a human in good order. We will never in a million years find another star to take Earth's place.

Worryingly, the corruption that so offended a young Dan Welty lives on fed by the heedless destruction of our only habitable planet by billionaires in league with the spawn of Pendergast - Putin, Modi, Bolsonaro, Duterte and Donald Trump. They choke our whales, birds, fish and corals with plastic and salt the land with chemicals a billion years' worth of life has never encountered.

Thanks dad. You were a good little Republican to worry about Boss Pendergast and his heirs. Little did you know that you were a RINO.

Harry Welty is a small town eccentric who paints more opinions than you could shake a stick at wherever he finds a boxcar on the Internet.

Collective Bargaining
Published Jan, 5, 2006

Back in my college days I was strictly a liberal arts kind of guy. I managed to get by with only four business classes and one of those was a typing course. Before I graduated, however, I wanted to take my dad's business law class.

My dad moved us to Minnesota after being passed over for a promotion in the Kansas State Insurance Commission. He'd suggested that his boss, the Commissioner, stop accepting gifts from the insurance companies he regulated. Becoming a college teacher insulated dad from the venal, "real world" and the terrible scandal that rocked the Insurance Commission a decade later.

My father was a strong believer that people learn best when they are fully engaged in a task and he liked games. He even invented a couple of board games and pitched them unsuccessfully to Parker Brothers. He thought competition and play were great lubricants for education and he made them an essential part of his law class. Students either flocked to his class or, if they were shrinking violets, shunned it.

He divided his students into two-person "law firms." Every day the firms argued contract case law with each other or sat in judgment of other cases being argued. Firms were assigned real suits that had already been settled. Half of the cases they were given had been won by plaintiffs and half by defendants. Firms that won more than fifty percent of their cases earned higher grades. Firms that lost more suffered.

Although preparing for the cases took time this part of the class was a breeze for me. I always argued the cases our firm was supposed to lose and generally won them. My partner argued the cases we were supposed to win and frequently won. Had this been the sole determinant of my grade I would have done well but there was one more assignment at the end of the semester that nearly unhorsed me.

Dad's class ended with a collective bargaining simulation during which half the firms represented labor and the other half management. I may have had a silver tongue but I had very little real world experience. All I knew about salaries and benefits was the minimum wage. To give these negotiations some real world punch dad built a potential calamity into it. If firms could not agree on a contract they forfeited all the collective bargaining points. Although strikes were rare they did occur and they weren't good for anyone's GPA.

My partner and I were assigned to represent a Mankato retailer. As it did not occur to me to find out what real world benefits amounted to (being a liberal arts kind of guy) I went into the negotiations blind. Unfortunately, my partner, who was a business major, was so taken with my debating skill and perhaps my kinship with the teacher that he deferred to me during our negotiations.

Our chief adversary was a fellow who looked more like an anarchist with his scruffy beard than a business major and he was not in awe of me or my connection to our teacher. If anything my being the teacher's kid gave him an extra impetus to drive a hard bargain and the threat of a strike gave him the perfect weapon. I don't know how serious he was about taking a strike but I had no doubt about the threat back then. Even so, I had no idea how much we had given away until I overheard my father grading the settlements. When he got to ours he groaned, "Oh my God!" Apparently the settlement we'd agreed to would have bankrupted the retailer. Thank goodness it was only a game.

There have been some profound changes in labor/management relations since I graduated. The most dramatic change has been the globalized market place which has undermined the once potent threat of a strike. "You want to strike? Go right ahead. We'll just take our factory to Asia where non-union workers will work for peanuts."

I don't wish to make any moral judgments about the world's new economy. Certainly, I'm happy that workers in the third world are getting the same kind of opportunities that Americans have long enjoyed. But I have a word of caution for the NAFTA loving politicians who have helped bring this new world about. Elections are won by majorities. As long as a majority of Americans can count on having jobs, pensions and medical benefits there is hope for the free traders.

To that end the free traders ought to encourage the establishment of strong unions in the third-world. If workers in the emerging world take advantage of the power to strike for their own benefits, safety and health it could help slow down the great "race to the bottom." If the race doesn't slow down the free traders will find themselves caught up in it as well.

Welty is a small time politician who lets it all hang out at: www.snowbizz.com

You Wanna Fight?

Published November 14, 2002

Harry 8th grade

Spoiler Alert Re: the following story
Harry survived seventh grade

I used to have a southern accent. I didn't say "ya'll" or anything like that because I was from Kansas . Still, I sounded different enough so that when my family moved to Minnesota the kids in my new junior high school called me "Reb." This nickname was not bestowed in kindly condescension.

All of the students in North Mankato Junior High had attended the same elementary school the previous year and I was the only new kid. The seventh grade's social elite was already clearly established. One particular alpha male carried himself with an assurance that was guaranteed to keep popular girls hanging around his locker. This was John.

I happened to sit in front of John in English. A week or so after school started I turned around to collect the homework that our row was passing forward to turn in. I don't think I did anything to provoke John while I waited for him to pass me the papers. Nonetheless, he narrowed his eyes and challenged me with cool arrogance. "You wanna fight me?"

"Sure," I lied, hoping and praying that he was just pulling my leg. The code of junior high bravado required the answer I had given John. He wasn't kidding. I took a mental gulp and asked him where and when we should meet. "At seven tonight. Under the traffic light at range and garfield."

After dinner I casually told my mother that I had to go. Puzzled, she asked me why. "Because I have to go fight a guy," Mom didn't argue with me and I don't recall her asking me a lot of questions. I knew she felt helpless in the face of this adolescent stupidity. She couldn't even defer to my father for guidance. He was still working back in Kansas. And besides, her own father had been a war hero. We lived in the age of Gary Cooper and High Noon. A man must do what a man must do.

It was dusk when I rounded the corner heading for the light at the appointed intersection. A gang of nine or ten guys were chasing around under the light. I'd have to fight John with a crowd to cheer him on or maybe worse.

"Is John here?" I asked as I drew near.

"No," one of the guys replied. "I think I saw him down by Range and Monroe ." Oh, I'd gotten the directions wrong. At least there wouldn't be a crowd.

"OK, Thanks," I replied, and began walking the two blocks toward the neighborhood store. But John wasn't there either. He was just taking his sweet time. I was sure that he would be back with the gang by the time I walked back.

"What do you want John for?" Wayne Schultz asked me after my return.

"John and I are supposed to have a fight." I said as nonchalantly as I could.

"Well, you can fight me instead," Wayne grinned. I swallowed my shock. "OK," I replied.

Wayne and I began circling. In an instant the gang circled us in turn and began cheering for Wayne.

I was reluctant to throw a punch. I'd never been in a real fight before. I knew about punch drunks whose brains had turned to mush in the boxing ring. I had no desire to do such damage to anybody. Fortunately, Wayne and I didn't come to blows. Instead, Wayne and I closed on each other and locked our arms around each other's head. We "wrassled." (I was from Kansas remember)

One of the gang, Dizzy, who would later be imprisoned for attempted rape, began kicking me in the butt while my upper body was otherwise engaged. I'm pretty sure he was aiming for something else. I did my best to keep my balance as Wayne and I grappled and danced for several furious minutes.

At some unspoken cue, Wayne and I unclenched while we were both still standing. Our "fight" was over. "Aw, you woulda beat John easy," said Wayne , "Cause I can take him."

Rarely have I felt such gratitude to anyone as I felt for Wayne Schultz that night. Neither of us were winners. Neither of us were losers. Wayne , as the local favorite, had helped me discharge my responsibility to manhood and left me with my dignity.

America hasn't always been as generous after its own battles. There was little of Lincoln 's "with malice toward none" following the Civil War. On the other hand America got a good look at European recriminations after the First World War and turned its back on the Old Country until their legacy of vengeance pulled us inexorably into the Second World War.

America was generous to Germany and Japan afterwards, perhaps to a fault. We needed a few of their scoundrels for the Cold War which followed. But more importantly we instituted the Marshall Plan. We are still collecting dividends from our magnanimity to this day.

I pray that if we should come to blows in Iraq we will remember the best lessons of our past. I am frankly nervous on this account. Our quick indifference to Afghanistan following our stunning victory there is not a good sign. I sure hope that we aren't so caught up in our short term addiction to SUV's and the good low-tax life to make a longer term investment in the future of these nations. I'd like them to remember us the same way I remember Wayne Schultz.

Harry Welty is a small time politician who lets it all hang out at: www.snowbizz.com

An older woman
Part 2, My 1972

Thursday Feb. 8th, 2024

In 1986 I got a classroom of seventh graders rolling on the floor laughing when I described how my three-year-old son climbed on a chair at Perkins and announced to the Sunday crowd, "I AM A BOY AND I HAVE A PENIS!" The laughing grew more frenzied when I told the class that my son loudly added, "MY DAD IS A MAN AND HE HAS A PENIS!"

In 1987, after an eighth grade girl called me a "douche" in class, I calmly asked her if she knew what a douche was. When she gave me a sly smile and shook her head "no" I told her a douche was a "vagina cleaner." I got fired for saying that.

Before he was President, Donald Trump went on a late night TV show, pulled a Trojan packet out of his coat pocket and yelled, "Safe sex, everyone!" Before he was elected most of us heard him say on tape, "I did try and f*** her, she was married."

Today his fervent evangelical voters think these are signs of a leader chosen by God to help them make theirs the official religion of America. They are getting closer. In states that make abortion nearly impossible, since the Dobbs decision there are 69,000 women who have pregnancies from rape.

This Christianity springs from the South where Sunday school classes were taken to the lynchings of accused black rapists. It makes me feel a responsibility to lay out how I learned about sex. So I will and BTW my example is more tame than some stories I know like the fraternity brother who bet he could bed a new woman every night for a month. He was obviously Presidential timber.

After 50 years there are fewer people for my candor to embarrass. The older woman I happily allowed to seduce me is long gone but her children are not so I'll be vague. Her age was roughly halfway between mine and my mother's.

When I was in junior high my Mom was just a little too eager to have me learn about the birds and the bees. Minnesota was a little ahead of most states and God fearing Christians opposed Sex-ed. My Mother feared my ignorance more than God. I was horrified when she asked if I was learning everything I needed to know. Of course I lied and said "sure." To be frank the teachers of 1964 were far less eager to talk about certain body parts than I was in 1987. For a long time I was just like them.

As a very small child I recall seeing my mother naked while she dressed. I probably stared at her too intently because I never again saw her naked. In fact, I became such a prude that I knew that if my baggy swim suit slipped off after I dived into a swimming pool I would have no choice but to commit suicide rather than face ridicule.

Despite my reticence my Mother was patient, clever and a good story teller. After my family left Topeka, Kansas for Minnesota she felt so guilty leaving her widowed father in a Topeka rest-home that she and her sister took turns driving to Kansas every month for week-long visits with their war hero father, George Robb. At every visit she would ask him about his past and she would bring that past back to me in what now seem to have been debriefings.

She wanted me to know that history. I was especially interested in stories about the First World War that resulted in my grandfather being awarded the nation's highest military honor. On one occasion she brought back a story about sex that piqued my interest.

In the trenches my grandfather's best friend was a fellow lieutenant. Lieut. Siebel was a worldly New Yorker. He would later be killed in a bomb blast that also killed their commanding officer and injured my grandfather. It was the first of three wounds grandfather suffered that day and each time he refused to go the aid station behind the trenches. He had a battle to fight.

Mom told me how the two men were debating whether it was better to have sex with a single woman or a married woman. The experienced Siebel told my grandfather it was better to have sex with a married woman because if she got pregnant there wouldn't be a scandal. Why it didn't occur to Siebel, whose soldiers were black Americans, that such secrets might not always be easy to hide I don't know. Perhaps race mixing was so inconceivable it didn't occur to him.

Grandfather must have been persuaded by his comrade because Mom told me how angry this made her. She told her father that impregnating a married woman could destroy a family. But on the other hand she also seemed to be defending single women. She told her father of a friend from college who had been sexually active. His view from 1918 was different from hers in 1948. Somehow without sex-ed she had learned ways of avoiding pregnancy. Maybe it had something to do with that strange rubber disc in our medicine cabinet

Mother wasn't finished with me because she put another idea in my head that didn't seem that far off from Lt. Siebel's advice. Mom told me that in medieval Europe well-to-do families introduced their sons to older women who would school them on sex. For some time this was simply theoretical. So, staying vague I will cut to the chase. My first "time" was with one of Lt. Siebel's older women although she was no longer married. She would throw snowballs at my window to alert me to join her.

Our first time I told her I didn't want to make her pregnant. She told me not to worry. No babies were conceived but not long afterward she warned me that she had been exposed to an STD meaning that I would have to be treated too.

As Trump told his TV audience, "Safe sex, everyone!"
There's no telling what Welty might say at lincolndemocrat.com

Christmas by George

Thursday Dec. 16th, 2021

One of Georganne Welty's first class of Christmas ornaments, 1981.

When I was in fourth grade my mom offered to help my teacher, Mrs. Knight, teach my classmates how to make puppets out of papier mâché. She had been making Christmas doves, angels and carolers from papier mâché for years.

Now with small kids she started making puppets.

The several days she spent helping us form and paint heads that would attach to cloth bodies were the most memorable of the year.

It was a great improvement over learning long division, which only drove me to break pencils in frustration.

Someone made Mrs. Knight a puppet theater like those for a Punch and Judy show or Kookla, Fran and Ollie. We could hide behind it, lift our puppets up in front of its curtain and ad-lib puppet shows.

I discovered voices and invented conversations that made my classmates laugh far harder than the jokes I told. Theater proved to be as compelling as basking in the glory of the other student's awe for my mother's project.

My mother had set her sights on becoming an artist from a very young age. As an eight-year-old she was crushed to discover that her father had covered up the calendar full of butterflies she had drawn for him under stacks of paper.

More distressing was finding the plaster skull that could hold pencils in its eye sockets prominently displayed on top of the pile of paper. This was her older sister's art and the paper weight was still around when I was a kid. It was pretty cool.

Mom was pursuing an art degree when she got married but she set aside her ambition and became a diaper-changing, baby-boom mother instead.

Making puppets was not the work of an abstract artist but it was a rewarding placeholder. It would be 10 years before she returned to college to finish her art degree. It would take five more before she found another place holder to test her skills.

In 1971 a group of "faculty wives" from Mankato State decided to start a "consignment" store. It would sell locally made goods and split the profits with the makers of corn stalk dolls and cribbage boards.

They named their store "Harpies Bazaar," riffing off of the woman's magazine Harper's Bazaar.

My mother nearly burst her buttons when she was asked to join, until she deduced her invitation had more to do with being married to an attorney. He could draw up the store's business documents much as another Harpies' husband in the Accounting department could handle their financial records and taxes.

My first and only contribution to the store was to help take down an earlier store's outdoor sign. Doing so unleashed 50 years of toxic sparrow's nest dust.

The Harpies soon discovered my mother's many talents. She had decorated store display windows when I was little. She illustrated hundreds of ads, for which the Mankato Free Press won an advertising award.

In 1981, the year our first child was born, she returned to papier mâché. She made Christmas ornaments that sold like hotcakes. She signed them all "by George."

They started simple but 13 years later they had become more fanciful, like the spindly-legged frog sitting on a cucumber that one of the Harpies' children found in their garden.

It wasn't painting, but my mother was having a marvelous time. Harpies Bazaar was everyone's favorite boutique in southern Minnesota. Rustic consignments gave way to the finest products the Harpies scouted out at huge merchandising conventions.

It was more a labor of love than a money-making proposition, although by Black Friday the Harpies could usually count on a modest profit.

My mother enjoyed one benefit. Harpies could purchase anything in the store "at cost." At Christmas my mother always trooped her children to the closed store at night to pick out whatever they (we) wanted for a bargain-basement price.

From 1981 to 1994 each Christmas season brought all new designs. The only break was in 1987 when my father died, and 1988 when mom moved to St. Paul after enrolling in the Minnesota Academy of Art and Design.

She was ready to become a real artist. After her graduation she rented an artist's loft and began painting abstract art so unlike her Christmas ornaments. Now she signed her canvases more soberly, "Georganne Welty."

Other than a passing interest in political cartooning I never fancied being an artist but I always wanted to show Mom my school art work. I was so aggravated the windy day that

Sherman took my portfolio and emptied it out on the school playground.

Thanks to my daughter, who once asked me to make a snow dinosaur, I followed my mother's artistic inclinations.

My medium is more fleeting than sawdust and flour paste but, like my mother, I get a lot of friendly feedback at Christmas.

Everything that Harry writes that is not about the imminent destruction of Earth as we knew it is superfluous. But, he does prattle on at lincolndemocrat.com.

WAR AND PEACE

America was born in war, using 'Indian' tactics because the enemy was better supplied and because the fighting colonists needed to return to their homes and families to get the next crop in, unlike most Red Coats and Hessians. America's failure to remember our example often pitted us against opponents who had learned from our success, thus keeping our superior forces at bay. Several 'conflicts' rivaled the eight years of the Revolutionary War, from the Battle of Bunker Hill to the signing of the Treaty of Paris. Sometimes we were as high-minded as the patriots; sometimes we were as stubborn as King George. My family lived through many such times.

George Robb shaking hands with President John F Kennedy in the
Rose Garden along with other recipients of a Medal of Honor.

Sergeant York
Published Jan. 2005

When I was in fifth grade my Grandfather made one of
his infrequent visits to our house. It was the only time that we
watched a movie together.

George Robb, my Mother's Father, was a man whose
example both my parents encouraged me to emulate. Since
Grandfather had been given the nation's highest military award,
the Congressional Medal of Honor (MOH), this would prove a
challenge.

MOH winners are few and exalted for their
"conspicuous gallantry above and beyond the call of duty."
Duluth has one, Mike Colalillo, and the City named a street in
his honor in West Duluth.

My grandfather was always appropriately modest about his MOH. He claimed that he hadn't done anything more heroic than countless others had done. When his award was announced shortly after his discharge from a military hospital he told the Army to mail it to him. The garrison near his home in Salina, Kansas, had other ideas. The Salina schools were closed for the award ceremony and Pathé films made a newsreel of the occasion for movie theaters.

I got to thinking about my grandfather's visit when my wife and I drew up an eclectic list of old movies to watch during the holidays. I put "Sergeant York" on the list.

Thirty years ago, before DVD's and VHS tapes, people watched whatever the three networks had to offer. Coincidentally "Sergeant York" was scheduled for broadcast during my grandfather's visit. My mother enthusiastically suggested that he stay and watch it with us and to our surprise he agreed.

My grandfather wasn't a fan of the movies. Perhaps, during the Depression, he regarded them as an extravagance. I tell of a rare exception in the column that follows this. George Robb had a master's degree in History. He had no truck with Hollywood's glamorized nonsense. But Sergeant York was a different movie. For one thing it was a great motion picture. It was filmed in 1941 on the eve of America's entry into the Second World War. In its own subtle way the movie helped pave the way for a reluctant America to break out of the isolationism and the national disillusionment brought on by the First World War.

In 1941 my grandfather was an isolationist. He was being consistent. In 1916 he had taken the unprecedented step of voting for a Democrat, Woodrow Wilson, because of his promise to keep America out of Europe's war. Yet my grandfather also lived by a simple credo "my country right or wrong." He volunteered immediately for the war he had so vigorously opposed.

My grandfather didn't watch the movie with us because of its reputation but because of its subject matter, Alvin York.

However modest my grandfather was about his own exploits he held the mysterious York in awe. While my grandfather attended many national reunions with other MOH winners he never met the modest and retiring York . Alvin York had been a reluctant warrior and this is the chief subject of the movie named after him.

A Tennessee farm boy, York had applied to be a conscientious objector after being drafted. According to the movie he believed that the Ten Commandments forbade the taking of human life so he fought to stay out of the Army. During the Vietnam War the Supreme Court would uphold CO status for men like York but during the First World War York's appeals were rejected. The movie is an earnest attempt to portray his remarkable shift from CO to MOH winner and his single-handed capture of 132 German soldiers.

My wife chuckled in disbelief as Gary Cooper, the movie's star, grimly marched his prisoners to the American lines in a near futile attempt to find someone who could cope with all his POWs. The story is true. It's in the citations.

My grandfather made no disparaging remarks about York , as he had after being pestered into seeing a movie about General Custer. The moral conundrums faced by York never troubled my grandfather. If a war is none of your business - stay out of it. Once someone has made it your business, win it. That was my grandfather's opinion. But York's story, Howard Hawks's movie, and my grandfather's admiration for York all left a deep impression on me.

I carried the memory of Sergeant York into the Vietnam Era. The movie inoculated me against pacifism but it never made me a devotee of "my country right or wrong." I expect America to be right.

Welty is a small time politician who lets it all hang out at: www.snowbizz.com

They died with their boots on

Thursday Mar. 3rd, 2022 Duluth Reader

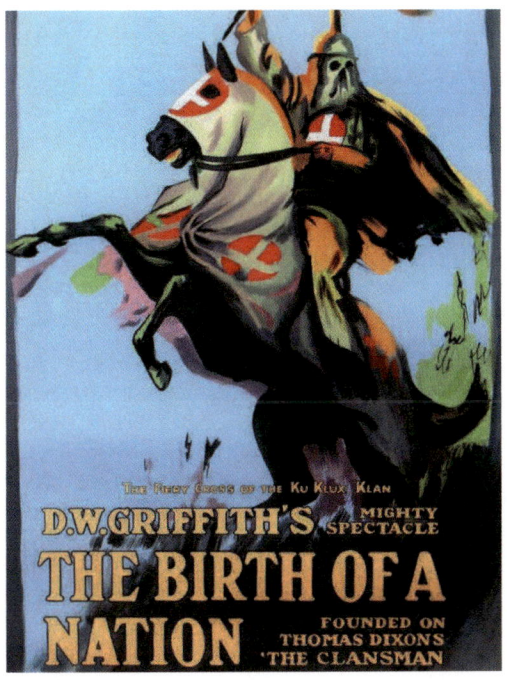

Hollywood spent its first 50 years cruelly confirming white America's every prejudice against black America. From their westerns you would never have known that one in three cowboys were former slaves.

Television kept up this all-white fiction. When I was a kid prime-time gun fighting was exclusively a white man's business. The only black you could find in Westerns were the bad guy's black hats.

My history-book-reading grandfather had no time for movies. While my dad's family sent their son to cowboy matinees; Hopalong Cassidy was dad's favorite because Hoppy didn't sing or kiss girls. Poor mom was movie deprived.

I wonder if 1915's movie Birth of a Nation (BOTN) had anything to do with his attitude. This Star Wars-caliber mega hit by director D. W. Griffith was a celebration of the blood-soaked Ku Klux Klan. It clocked in at an astonishing 3 hours and 7 minutes. Four years later it still enjoyed huge audiences all across America but it was introduced in New York City, where, coincidentally, my grandfather was studying for his masters degree in History.

Columbia University sat across the street from Harlem, which was then undergoing its "Black Renaissance." A very different renaissance was underway among Columbia's history faculty. Under the direction of my grandfather's teacher, Professor William A. Dunning, Columbia was rewriting the nation's textbooks to confirm Birth of a Nation's story of the Civil War's aftermath.

Black audiences were horrified and fought a heartfelt battle to kill the movie much as today some are fighting deep fake Internet tropes. In 1915 they were stopped cold by the First Amendment.

Meanwhile, white audiences fell in love with BOAN. In the following years the KKK would achieve its highest national membership.

I don't know if my 28-year old grandfather saw the movie. I suspect he was largely immune from his professor's revisionist story line that the South bravely turned the tables on northern carpetbaggers and shiftless, freed men. It was a fantasy that probably had Ulysses S Grant rolling in his famous tomb, across from the Columbia campus.

My grandfather deeply admired Grant. My mother gave her father's copy of Grant's autobiography to my son. It had been owned by his father, who proudly called himself a "black Republican." That sobriquet was one of the South's contemptuous names for "N lovers." The Robb family's next-door-neighbor, Larry Lapsley, had escaped slavery during the Civil War.

There was no greater fan of Birth of a Nation than the Georgia-born President, Woodrow Wilson. The President showed it in the White House and proclaimed it the truest depiction of Reconstruction. He would go on to segregate the civil service, which had the effect of gutting its black work force.

Birth of a Nation had a whitewashed successor in Hollywood's next blockbuster, 1939's Gone with the Wind. In glorious technicolor GWTW lasted almost an hour longer than BOAN at three hours and 58 minutes. Although he read the book I doubt George Robb ever went to see the movie.

My mother's older sister thought of a sure-fire sales pitch to convince their father to take them to a movie in 1941. They wanted to see Errol Flynn's dashing portrayal of General Armstrong Custer in the shoot-em-up, They Died with Their Boots On. It was history, they told their father. It would be educational. My grandfather grudgingly took them to see the Sioux Indians cut the gallant Seventh Calvary to pieces. After it was over Georganne and Mary Jane breathlessly asked their father what he thought of the movie. He was curt. "Custer should have been court-martialed."

In his own quiet way my Grandfather would argue against the prejudices his Ivy League profs bequeathed to Hollywood and spread across America. Two years out of Columbia he became a white officer leading black soldiers from Harlem in France. He would later write glowing accounts of their courage.

But he would be swimming against a heavy tide. As he lay recuperating from his war wounds during 1919 white vigilantes started 27 "major" white on black race riots killing hundreds. During the war blacks had taken white jobs in the North; came back as veterans thinking they deserved some respect and tried to move into white neighborhoods.

Who did they think they were? Hadn't they seen themselves in Birth of a Nation?

After the Second World War Hollywood cautiously began pulling its knife from the back of black America.

Bahamian actor Sidney Poitier was its point man. He gave color to The Defiant Ones, Lilies of the Field, A Patch of Blue and In the Heat of the Night.

But things have gone too far for the new Lincoln-Free Republican Party. The legislatures it controls are bent on protecting the ignorance of such people as the old white lady who screamed at a black employee at Mount Vernon National Park. The black employee told her that her job was to play the part of one of President Washington's slaves. The old lady screamed at her that George Washington never owned slaves.

Republicans are so agitated with the teaching of honest black history, that they have written laws to monitor history teachers with body-cams like the police to keep them politically correct. Some have even held book burnings.

They also have an affinity with Vladimir Putin. Putin hates hearing anything bad about his idol Joseph Stalin. If he can just win the Ukraine back maybe they will forget that Stalin starved 4 million of them before Hitler swept in and killed another couple million and made the rest slave laborers.

Maybe Putin will even help them forget that Stalin shipped the surviving slave laborers to die in his Gulags for being "Nazi collaborators."

Yeah. Putin has the right idea – the Republican idea.

Everything Harry writes that is not about the imminent destruction of Earth as we knew it is superfluous. But, he does prattle on at lincolndemocrat.com.

My Vietnam
May 24, 2018

Peace Sign cuff links made by Harry Welty's Uncle Frank, a Korean War Veteran

I just read a short biographical story about Robert Mueller III which described how he earned a bronze star and a purple heart in Vietnam. The story briefly contrasted Mueller and the draft-dodging Donald Trump. It described how Trump has often joked that avoiding STD's in the 1980's was "his Vietnam," and how his constant pursuit of sex marked him as very brave soldier. Both men are five years my senior and reached draft age before the war turned sour.

I had my own Vietnam experience and Like Trump's it was back here in the states. "My Vietnam" began when I learned what to expect from my mother when I skinned a knee. She told me, "Don't cry Harry. Your grandfather was shot" (as a soldier in World War 1) "and he didn't cry."

As you have or will read throughout these pages I learned at a tender age that that his heroics in that war brought my Grandfather honor and celebrity.

Grandfather was certain that the United States had no business fighting in a European war. Despite this my Grandfather could not abandon his credo "my country right or wrong." He was among the first to enlist and in doing so he gave up a safe job as a high school principal. Long after his war time convalescence he would continue to blame Democrats Franklin Roosevelt and Harry Truman for getting us into new wars all of which sprung from Wilson's broken promise.

When I began seventh grade another democrat, Lyndon Johnson, was getting us mired in Vietnam. My Father, a World War II vet, was outraged. He cussed out LBJ at every announcement of increasing troop shipments during the evening news. Donald Trump, was also John Kerry's age. Kerry, a 2004 presidential contender, was a Democrat and like my grandfather a man of duty. He enlisted and fought in the Mekong River. I can't help but wonder where the Republican patriots who "swift boated" John Kerry were when the randy, draft-dodger Trump was campaigning to become our Nation's Commander-and-Chief.

Enrolling in college gave me a four-year student deferment from Vietnam when I was draft bait with a low draft number of #41. Like my Republican father I opposed the war and yet I could not put my grandfather's example out of my head especially when I saw a nincompoop burn his draft card in my first few days of college. That's coming up next in "**About a Corn Cob**.

By the time I got to college we had a Republican President and one who may have secretly prolonged the Vietnam War by sabotaging the Paris Peace Talks when he ran for President. It was during the Nixon Administration's *Republican* War that I turned my back on "My Country Right or Wrong." I would only accept my Country's being right.

I began playing the contrarian during those college years. When a group of students marched to occupy our college President's offices I laid down on the sidewalk in front of their march and forced them to step over me. A few of the saints pointedly dragged their feet across my chest.

In 1972 I gladly voted for Democrat George McGovern, a much maligned "Peace" Democrat for President while turning up my nose at working for the well healed Nixon reelection campaign. And yet, when the McGovern campaign challenged a desiccated College Republican club to a debate I took up the challenge of defending Richard Nixon in front of hundreds of rabid Nixon haters. I did it out of the democratic conviction that everyone deserved an advocate. When, after the debate, two good friends told me that they were disappointed in me I offered no self-justification. If they wanted to be disappointed in me that was their prerogative.

My patriot grandfather was disheartened with the anti-war protests of my generation and the peace marches I gladly joined so long as they weren't staged like middle fingers. I lucked out of Vietnam graduating the year soldiers began coming home but I took no joy in having avoided the military.

By remaining a civilian I had a lot of company. A lot of Republican company.

That was our Vietnam.

Harry Welty is a small-time politician who also pontificates at www.lincolndemocrat.com

About a Corn Cob
Published Feb 19, 2004

I just read Newsweek's evenhanded account of the war years of George Bush and John Kerry. (Feb 23, 2004) Although these gentlemen are five and seven years older than me, respectively, we were all caught up in Vietnam, our nation's longest running war. In 1968, the year Bush graduated from college to the National Guard, John Kerry was patrolling the Mekong Delta. It was the year of the Tet Offensive, the Mai Lai massacre and the assassinations of anti-war candidate Robert Kennedy and anti-war critic Martin Luther King Jr. It was also the year my crusty old American Lit teacher told our class that his comrades-in-arms had never cut the ring fingers off of the enemy's dead for souvenirs. I was a high school junior.

I didn't need Mr. Haugen's persuasion to oppose the Vietnam War. For four years I had heard my own father, another WW II vet, cuss out Lyndon Johnson every time the President deployed more troops to Vietnam .

In my senior year I drew number 41 out of 365 in the draft lottery. Thanks to a student deferment the only thing standing between me and the military was four years of college. That gave me four years to protest the war *and I would protest!*

After my senior year I worked Minnesota's "corn pack." I was put on a line that sent pallets of sweet corn cobs to be flash frozen. There were fifteen or twenty of us from Mankato. We were picked up at daybreak and bussed 25 miles to Waseca's *Birds Eye* plant. There we joined Waseca kids, farm wives and Mexican migrants on a ten hour day not counting the two-way bus ride. It wasn't particularly hard work but it was a damn long day.

There was a whiff of resentment between the Waseca boys and the Mexicans who moved into their town every summer. Fortunately, the Waseca kids and the migrant kids minded their own business and socialized separately during breaks.

One of the Mankato kids was a tall beanpole of a kid a couple years older than me. I hadn't known him because he had attended Mankato State's "laboratory" high school where ambitious parents sent their kids to give them a superior education. He wore army fatigues and sported a scraggly beard like Che Guevara's.

One day "Che" was bored and decided to liven things up. He whipped a loose corn cob at the back of one of the Waseca boys, an alpha male, nailing him on the head. Pleased with his marksmanship Che turned around and chuckled into his hand so the victim wouldn't notice him. I'm sure that most of the Mexican kids on our line saw Che do the dirty deed. None of us was willing to break the pan-cultural taboo against ratting out a troublemaker, however, so we all continued working.

The Alpha male grabbed his head and glared at the Mexicans on our line. It only took him an instant to fix on the person he was sure had insulted him. He charged over to our line, followed by his friends, his gaze locked on one of the Mexican kids. As a circle of hostile Mexicans and Wasecans formed on the factory floor Che was doubled over in mirth. The warring parties were so intent on defending their honor that they were oblivious to the bemused Che.

Unlike the Vietnam War our Mexican standoff blew over quickly. Someone stepped in and put an end to it. It's not surprising that I've forgotten how the fight ended because an anticlimax is, by self-definition, unmemorable. No one ever fingered Che.

A few weeks later I began college. War protests, although in their infancy, were beginning to make the leap from the nation's elite universities to state colleges. I would soon join a peace march that would block Mankato's main intersection and royally irritate drivers who could not understand how being forced to take detours would end the Vietnam War.

The first week of class I walked past a circle of curious onlookers surrounding a student who was burning his draft card. It was Che, the corn cob provocateur, dressed in his khaki finest. Within the year Che would break into a Draft Board office and burn selective service files. He would be convicted for his crime and thus become an anti-war martyr. He was sent to a mental hospital.

Over the last thirty years I have had many occasions to watch people like Che on both sides of the political spectrum. A lot of these folks are having a high old time now that we are in Iraq. Keep an eye out for flying corn cobs.

Welty is a small time politician who lets it all hang it at: www.snowbizz.com

'We will not have another Kent State in Mankato' My 1972 Pt 4

Thursday Feb. 15th, 2024

One of my first columns for the Reader in 2002 was "You Wanna Fight" about my introduction to Minnesota in seventh grade. I was challenged to a fight and its one of my favorite stories because in hindsight it seems so Lincolnesque.

While I grappled with Wayne, another kid I'll call Dizzy was in the circle of cheering boys that surrounded us playing the part of Fox News. While I was in a headlock with Wayne Schultz, the hero of my story, Dizzy was busy trying to kick my family jewels. Dizzy was such a pill that a cousin of his once told me he was embarrassed to share the same name.

Dizzy never bothered me again but I kept a wary eye on him as he spiraled down in life. My Dad told me after I was safely married and living in Duluth that Dizzy had been sent to prison for attempted rape.

The last time I remember seeing Dizzy, he was walking on the sidewalk near my house on May 9, 1972. He was obviously intoxicated but by what or what combination of things I could only guess. He was heading in the direction of the next day's headlines – the takeover of Highway 169 by Vietnam War protesters. The blockade was at the junction of Mankato and North Mankato over the Minnesota River.

I was headed uphill to Mankato State's upper campus, where a short time later I would find myself on the phone with the college intern for Congressman Nelsen, who took up where

I left off after my summer with Ancher. She was a saccharine sweet college Republican female version of the Oliphant cartoon character I displayed in my column "1972" a few weeks ago.

I had just parked myself in the sudent senate office where a radio broadcast was describing the kids headed over to block vehicles, including an ambulance at work.

I rather enjoyed relaying the play by play to the serious young woman knowing she would relay the story to the staff I had gotten to know. They were sure to be scandalized by the news, just as they had been outraged at the rude treatment of Senator Goldwater when he answered questions from lefty summer interns.

I didn't think this protest was too cool. In the Fall of 69 I'd watched an irate motorcycle rider run over the legs of a protester blocking an intersection two blocks shy of the highway. In my view, these actions only served to piss off potential allies. Suspecting that Dizzy was headed there did nothing to reconcile me to the ruckus.

While I was on the phone with Washington a second group of protesters were going to imitate the big leagues, or rather the Ivy league, protesters. They were on their way to take over the office of our college President James Nickerson.

This annoyed me and I decided to inflict a little reverse psychology on them by pulling a Gandhi. When I saw them leave the Student Union I raced ahead of them past a dormitory and parked myself for a lie down on the sidewalk. They would have to step over me on their way to protester nirvana. Several of them made a special point of dragging their feet across my chest. Police who did things like that were often called pigs.

President Nickerson left his office rather than confront the strident heroes. Years later he wrote a book about these turbulent days which I've consulted online. Much of it comes from the recollections of dozens of people who experienced the protests from different vantage points.

One of the contributors was the late Larry Spencer, who was the student senate president at the time.

They were all on a speaker phone with Governor Wendell Anderson's Chief of Staff Tom "I-holiday-in-Las-Vegas-and-always-win-lots-of-money-at-the-tables" Kelm.

Kelm scared the bejesus out of just about everybody in St. Paul. He put on a demonstration of aggression with Nickerson and his presidential cabinet, which included Student Senate President Spencer and the faculty union president, my Dad.

I had been listening to the "conservative" Daniel Welty, for years as he cussed out Lyndon Johnson every time more soldiers were sent off to Vietnam.

The call with the governor's office was about dealing with the march and the human blockade of Highway 169. Later my Father would fly out to DC to meet with Congressmen Nelsen so as to give him a picture of sentiment on the campus, and while he was at it mention his son the recent intern.

There was more to come for Mankato. Not long afterward someone planted a bomb and destroyed a newly constructed law enforcement center in the city.

On the speaker phone Kelm was channeling Chicago's hard-ass Mayor Daley as Nickerson's cabinet argued with him to back off from a confrontation with the students on the Bridge.

Here's Spencer's recollection of the call:

"Kelm had another plan in mind and said the governor would not endorse any civil disobedience, and that he was prepared to order out the National Guard to clear the highway and establish order. Dan Welty, a conservative Republican, broke the stunned silence after Kelm's threat by stating passionately, 'My God, my son is on that bridge. We will not have another Kent State in Mankato.'"

My Dad was mistaken. I was sure the blockade was going to give the peace movement a black eye, with guys like Dizzy drunkenly throwing beer bottles around. I'd just performed my own blockade of the protesters heading to take over Nickerson's office.

While it wasn't me who had anything to fear from the Governor's Chief of Staff my future wife was in harm's way. She had left Mankato High in high dudgeon over the war. She would have been in the line of fire.

Next week: the next day May 10th and my kind of protest march.

Harry Welty does this and that at lincolndemocrat.com

Tecla Karpen's Compliment
Duluth Reader Feb. 22, 2024

The children of Willie and Joe gave us flower power, marijuana and their father's college ambitions while being no more enamored of war than their fathers had been.

May 10th would bring a more sober protest march that would begin on the upper campus of Mankato State College.

The Baby Boom children needed educating. I recall reading somewhere that at our entry into the Second World War, following the Depression and the New Deal, only 1 in ten

Americans had graduated from high school.

When their father's returned from war sober American leaders decided the GIs deserved a fitting reward while helping America step up its game as the new undisputed leader of the world. The men who had stormed the beaches of Normandy and Iwo Jima were offered the GI Bill. Rumpled but reliable GIs like cartoonist Bill Maudlin's Willie and Joe would be rewarded by the nation in a most surprising way. The Nation would pay for the unimaginable - their college educations. Of course their children would follow them and do so impressively especially as the draft kicked in while a less black and white war beckoned high school grads to the steamy booby-trapped filled rice paddies of Vietnam. Young men could postpone bullets for four years in college. The 2-S deferment that waited for me from eighth grade through my college graduation - nine endless years - was probably on my Dad's mind every time he cussed out LBJ's troop deployments.

MSC's Upper Campus had just broken ground when we moved to Mankato in 1963. Two titanic ten-story dormitories stood there surrounded by corn fields. When I got to the campus in 1969 a dozen buildings could hold Mankato State's 15,000 students. The enrollment was double the size of North Mankato on the other side of the Minnesota River.

On this day 2000 of the GI's children were taking a break from fueling further economic growth. They had gathered to march for peace protesting the secret and illegal bombing of Cambodia. This was a far cry from the lone draft card burner I watched on my first week of class a few years earlier. I'd met the fellow during corn pack and saw him damn near start a race riot in the Birds Eye plant. I was not impressed. Look up: "About a corn cob" in "Snowbizz.com".

MSC students weren't particularly militant. A few students had traveled to Washington DC to march past Richard Nixon's White House and the Pentagon. They carried no Jan 6th guns and made no Jan 6th attempt to force their way into the corridors of power. One of them was the Student Senate President Larry Spencer who recalled my Father's ominous words about Kent State where young National Guardsman shot young protesters killing four. Unlike the previous day's bridge takeover this day's march would do the peace movement proud.

A temporary platform had been erected next to the Student Union with a half dozen folding chairs, a microphone and seated dignitaries appointed by God knows who. News cameras were at the ready to report on the day. They had also been on Highway 169 the previous day recording clouds of tear gas and broken beer bottles.

As we waited I kept my eye on a small collection of peace hoodlums sitting directly in front of the podium. I'd had words with one of them a few days before. Someone began speechifying at the mike and the audience listened to words of terrible gravity. When the small collection had heard enough they stood suddenly and screamed for a reporter to explain why he had made them look bad by filming beer cans and debris on the previous day. One reporter got up hesitantly to explain himself to two thousand people. But at his first syllable the peace-nicks screamed insults and drowned him out.

As I stood listening at the back of the audience rage welled up inside of me and I shouted at the top of my lungs "SHUT UP YOU SONS A BITCHES AND LET THE MAN SPEAK!" Startled, they shut up. Given this repreive the harried reporter said simply. I just reported what I saw. Now the crowd could march.

It was one of the most satisfying moments of my life. It was made all the sweeter when my college speech teacher Tecla Karpen walked over to me in awe and told me "I wish I'd been the one to say that." I've always considered that the finest compliment I've ever received.

The march through town was uneventful and probably got less coverage than the previous days shenanigans. I wouldn't go on a march again for another 45 years. Then in September of 2017 a year after Donald Trump assumed the Presidency and made it clear he had no use for science, women or civil rights I marched in three Duluth marches, one for each of these causes as did many other Americans throughout the nation.

There were no broken windows, beaten policeman or violence. No one hid their guns from metal detectors as they did on January 6th when Trump's orders not to set up metal detectors were ignored before he sent his supporters to the Nation's Capital to beat the hell out of our Capital Police.

For six months before the 2020 election with election polls predicting he was about to lose Trump began planning to declare a stolen election and to refuse to leave the White House. This is just what the Washington Post reported on June 22, 2020 long before the November election. I posted their story on my blog and asked, **"When Trump denies losing can we trust Pete Stauber to defend our democracy?"** (Feel free to Google it.)

The answer to my question was an emphatic and sycophantic **"NO."** Congressman Stauber has grown too comfortable with the lint in Donald Trump's pocket. He played dead.

And because I've been stewing about it for three years let me add that my former colleague on the School Board, Art Johnston, aided and abetted Trump's fraud when he too claimed that his election for the legislature that year was stolen.

Welty marches for good causes at:lincolndeocrat.com

Spitting on Bill
Published April 18, 2003

After the Vietnam War I read news stories about servicemen who were spat on when they returned to the United States. The stories were anecdotal and a few years later I read an opinion column that said these stories were all fabrications. I wanted to believe this because, whatever the follies of our foreign policy, servicemen were the wrong people to blame.

When I turned eighteen on December 10, 1968, my lottery number was fixed at 41. I could have been cannon fodder because the draft was in full swing but I was lucky. Our Congress had rigged the system so that boys who attended college got college draft deferments. This deferment improved on an idea from earlier wars that a fighting America couldn't imperil its war effort by drafting farmers and men who performed certain vital occupations. By the time of the Vietnam War college educations were deemed vital to the nation's security. Coincidentally, most Congressmen's sons attended college.

My dad, a World War II veteran, felt we had no business in Vietnam. He didn't think America had a strategic interest there. He doubted the "Domino theory." He fretted about a land war in Asia . He especially didn't want his son to be sent off to die in Vietnam just so some damn politicians wouldn't have to admit that they'd made a big mistake. I was in junior high when I first heard him cuss out Lyndon Johnson for sending more troops to Indochina. I was in college when I participated in my first anti-Vietnam War protest march.

The United States eventually did pull out of Vietnam, ingloriously. In doing so we shamefully left tens of thousands of Hmong and Vietnamese friends behind to fend for themselves after the North Vietnamese overran the country. Unlike earlier generations of veterans, dispirited Vietnam Era servicemen got no welcome and no thanks when they came back home. Despite the cocky dismissal in that Op Ed piece some veterans were spit on, including Bill, who sings with me in our church choir.

Bill never saw action in Vietnam but he saw more than enough of the consequence of war. He was a military dentist who helped rebuild the broken faces of young soldiers suffering from traumatic combat injuries. Some of these damaged young men had volunteered to save a foreign people from tyranny. Some had been drafted, as I might have been, and had no choice other than comply or flee to Canada. Whether the

Vietnam War was folly or not, these soldiers weren't to blame for it yet some of them were spit on when they returned.

Bill didn't take his uniform off quite fast enough. After he was spit on a superior officer encouraged him to remove his uniform and blend back into the civilian population. Bill smiled when he told me this story but it was the steely smile of a man recalling a cruel indignity. Bill's experience helps explain the bitter and, I think, wrong-headed denunciations of today's anti-Iraq War protesters.

I'm glad that America has a spirited Peace community but I have to shake my head at some of our anti-war protesters. There has been a foolish strain of peace-at-any-price idealism ever since World War II. Traumatized by the vast and pointless slaughter of the First World War these idealists were willing to cede the Sudetenland to Adolf Hitler to avoid war. Some of their descendants today seem intent on blaming the United States for the destruction of the World Trade Towers.

While I can find plenty of fault with America's foreign policy I still believe that America has been a force for good in the world. I am a little taken aback by those who are mortally offended by America's military. After all, our soldiers, sailors and marines have fought for freedom and democracy. They have put an end to the reign of tyrants and liberated concentration camps. They have done these things at great personal sacrifice.

Five years ago, as students from Duluth 's NJROTC program presented the American flag at a school board meeting, a Board colleague walked out of the room evidently offended by what she regarded as a display of militaristic nationalism.

Over the past month I've wondered whether any of the young people who presented the flag to us at that meeting were sent to Iraq. I've also wondered whether my colleague would be so quick to turn away in disgust if any of our former students were brought back home in flagged draped coffins.

Welty is a small time politician who lets it all hang out at www.snowbizz.com

NOTE: After publishing the previous column there was a row about whether the walkout took place. I would not be repeating this column if I had any doubts. If it did I can't be sure of anyone's motivations.

Emperors of lies
Thursday Mar. 17th, 2022

Vladimir Putin says the West is an "empire of lies." If this is so, a lot of them sprang from Putin's thought police and Internet trolls. Even Putin's top diplomat, the leaden-faced Foreign Minister Sergei Lavrov, blamed a Ukrainian maternity hospital's bombing on "Nazis."

A jealous Donald Trump is in awe at Putin's power to stifle the truth. Trump can only call factual reporting "fake news." Putin controls the press. There is no Ukrainian invasion. Anyone who says otherwise will spend 15 years in prison. God only knows what they would get if they reported the gross incompetence of their corrupt military.

Putin even sent in mobile crematoriums to hide the Russian dead from his people. But incompetence can only be hidden for so long. Now Putin has been forced to wave nuclear weapons in the face of every Earthling whether animal, vegetable or artificial intelligence.

Their use would leave even his erstwhile ally China a smoldering ruin.

The Ukraine Adventure is not Putin's first genocidal war. His first in the 1990's leveled the rebellious Chechen province. Hardly an apartment building was left standing. After his drug soaked celebration of peace at the Sochi Olympics he attacked the nation of Georgia. Then he pried the Crimea away from the Ukraine.

Then he experimented with thermobaric bombs to kill uncounted thousands in Syria's civil war. He has spent the last decade nibbling away at the Ukraine. But the nation Volodymyr Zelenskyy was elected to lead is the size of France with 44 million people not tiny Chechnya's one million.

I began writing this column as a world-wide performance of Ludwig von Beethoven's masterpiece the Ninth Symphony was playing to honor the people of the Ukraine.

Beethoven once imagined that Napoleon was bringing freedom to the people of Europe. He was profoundly angry to see that Bonaparte simply wanted to build an empire.

The next European revolution brought about the Soviet Union, a "worker's paradise," to end the evils of capitalism. But Stalin brought only death.

Hitler didn't promise a better world just a pure German empire.

Putin is following in his predecessors' footsteps with no sham claim to make a better world. He, like the "Aryan" Hitler, only wants a bigger empire for Russians.

Now that this future seems to be slipping through his fingers he seems driven by a motive no more compelling than, "If I can't have her no one can." Flattened maternity wards testify to his fury.

Putin can flatten much more than the Ukraine. Long after the 1962 Missile Crisis and the fall of the Iron Curtain a Russian general told an American counterpart how Russia could have flattened America with just nine nuclear-tipped missiles. Russia would go on to build 10,000 of them. Putin still has 6,000.

Former Republican presidential candidate Reverend Pat Robertson recently spoke for God telling his television audience that it's God's plan to let Putin destroy Earth. He's more articulate than Trump and saner than a lot of other Republicans.

Some believe that Donald Trump is an Old Testament king. Others believe Hillary Clinton organized a ring of pedophiles at a pizzeria. Others want a race war.

All of these and more believe everything Donald Trump says and some, like Fox News's Tucker Carlson, are quoted on Putin's Russian television.

Though I am an agnostic I have often sung a hymn based on the Ninth Symphony's final movement at my church. The hymn's lyrics seem appropriate to the moment:

Joyful, joyful, we adore You,

God of glory, Lord of love;

Hearts unfold like flow'rs before You,

Op'ning to the sun above.

Melt the clouds of sin and sadness;

Drive the dark of doubt away;

Giver of immortal gladness,

Fill us with the light of day!

All Your works with joy surround You,

Earth and heav'n reflect Your rays,

Stars and angels sing around You,

Center of unbroken praise;

Field and forest, vale and mountain,

Flow'ry meadow, flashing sea,

Chanting bird and flowing fountain

Praising You eternally!

Always giving and forgiving,

Ever blessing, ever blest,

Well-spring of the joy of living,

Ocean-depth of happy rest!

Loving Father, Christ our Brother,

Let Your light upon us shine;

Teach us how to love each other,

Lift us to the joy divine.

Mortals, join the mighty chorus,

Which the morning stars began;

God's own love is reigning o'er us,

Joining people hand in hand.

Ever singing, march we onward,

Victors in the midst of strife;

Joyful music leads us sunward

In the triumph song of life.

God bless the Ukraine!

PARTY OF LINCOLN

This is the snow sculpture Harry made in 2006 to announce he was leaving the Republican Party. He said he was taking Lincoln with him. He enjoyed his time with Democrats who made it clear they liked Lincoln but after getting Obama elected Harry thought the GOP needed Lincoln back. Sadly, the snow sculptor has only sculpted Abe twice and his antithesis Donald Trump three times.

Republicans were often a party that complained that history was no longer being taught to American students. Now, they disagree with historians. I'm sorry that the recent 2024 rankings which follow are so fuzzy.

This graph shows how American historians currently rank our presidents in terms of greatness. It's hard to read.

Figure 1: Presidential Greatness By Rank and Ratings

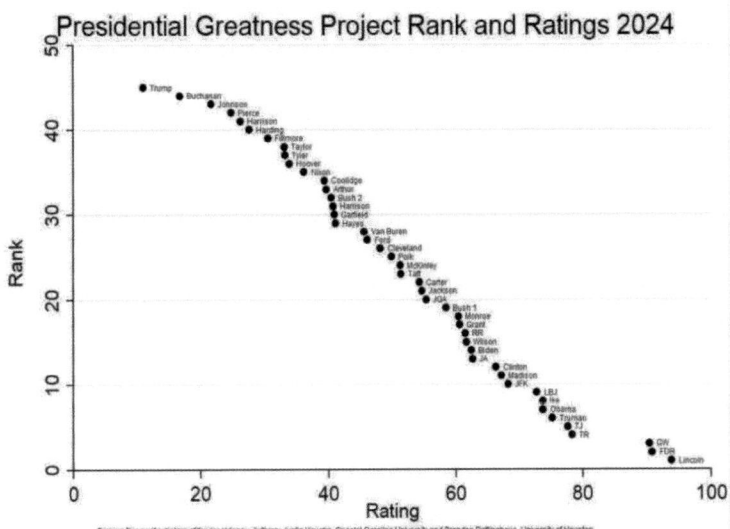

Source: Survey of scholars of the presidency. Authors: Justin Vaughn, Coastal Carolina University and Brandon Rottinghaus, University of Houston

At the top of this graph on the far left Trump is dead last. Lincoln, at the bottom right is first with a greatness rating of 92%. He wasn't perfect but he was damn good. FDR and Washington are not far behind him. Trump has been in the headlines since the defeat he has called a "steal." He will almost certainly be the Republicans next presidential nominee even if he succumbs to dementia like his father Fred. Incapacity allowed the son to rewrite his father's will and improve his inheritance at the expense of his deceased older brother. His niece took him to court and restored her share of the inheritance.

Trump has a habit of treating Americans like he treated his niece. He took over the brawling party that Lincoln used to bring the nation back together. Trump has given it a hive mind to cheer him on, as talk grows of a new Civil War:

The fall of Lincoln (#2)

Thursday Oct. 22nd, 2020

    A week ago angry protesters knocked down statues of two of my favorite presidents. It happened on the day set aside by Congress to let Italians know they were finally considered white. Teddy Roosevelt and Abe Lincoln both suffered from a condition known as being human. They had no access to Dr. Who's tardis to teleport them into a gentler future to see the errors of our past. That said, it could be argued that Teddy imagined a future where the environment would be treasured and Abe saw a future where the words "all men (and women) are created equal" would be taken seriously.

    The historian in me can forgive this trespass against my heroes. Pushing over a couple bronzes is hardly the end of the Republic. Our challenge might simply be to better learn the past so as to distinguish between slave owning traitors and our better angels.

I don't feel nearly so charitable towards the Republican successors who abandoned their party's founders. Republican Texas rewrote school text books to teach young Texans that it wasn't slavery that sparked the Civil War but federal interference in the state's economies. I'm sure Abe has been rolling in his grave ever since. The state's 1861 "Declaration of Causes" explaining its secession defends slavery paragraph after paragraph including this charming run-on sentence: "…We hold as undeniable truths that the … various states … were established exclusively by the white race, for themselves and their posterity, that the African race … were rightly held and regarded as an inferior and dependent race … " And Texas Republicans delight in spreading their toxic history.

Because Texas buys every school district's text books it requires textbook publishers to write Texas's warped view into history books. Because publishers salivate to make this huge sale they embed Texas claptrap into textbooks for the entire nation to propagandize every school child. Texas wants American children to see the world the way Rush Limbaugh says it works.

Republicans began abandoning Lincoln to pursue southern votes after I moved to Minnesota from Kansas in 1963. The Civil War's Centennial was in the news then as was Martin Luther King Jr. My new schoolmates called me "Reb" for my Kansas accent. The next year Arizona's Republican Senator Barry Goldwater ran for President but only won the South's electoral votes. He earned them by opposing the Civil Rights Act of 1964. My Republican parents voted Democrat for the first time in their lives. In 1968 Richard Nixon poached George Wallace, "segregation now, segregation tomorrow, segregation forever," voters to win the Presidency. And in 1980 Ronald Reagan conspicuously announced his presidential campaign in Neshoba County where sixteen years earlier the college kids

Chaney, Goodman and Schwerner were murdered for helping to register Mississippi's black voters.

But Donald Trump trumped them all in his bid for the Republican Presidential nomination by jetting around the nation with his preposterous claim that President Obama was a Kenyan and not an American. In his bid to stay in office, he came to Bemidji, Minnesota a couple weeks ago and told an audience of Aryans that they had good genes unlike Minnesota's Somali population. So much for the Preamble to the Declaration of Independence. AND that's not the half of it. Trump has told us that he's been a better president than Lincoln or George Washington. He also thinks he's entitled to an unconstitutional third term. The Republican party of my youth would have demanded that Trump take a psych evaluation. Which leads me to the lap dog I challenged in the recent Republican primary, Congressman Pete Stauber.

There has been no daylight between Stauber and Donald Trump. Nowhere has that been more stark than on Republican Party's calamitous handling of the corona virus. Three weeks short of the election Dr. Michael Osterholm, the director of the Center for Infectious Disease, has warned that: "the next six to 12 weeks are going to be the darkest of the entire pandemic." Maskless Pete just flew into Duluth on Air Force One with President Trump's infection tour.

The Republicans who saved the union would be dumbstruck by the divisions their southernized successors are sowing today. When I attended my first meeting in a short lived experiment to be a Democrat I was delighted that they made a big deal out of Abraham Lincoln. I trust them to tell our nation's history to the angry youngsters who pushed Abe and Teddy over in Portland. And it makes it easy for me to throw my support to Quinn Nystrom for Congress. I'll be one of her "RepubliQuinns"

The contrast with Pete is stark. Pete will help Donald Trump kill the Affordable Care Act. Quinn Nystrom organized bus trips to Canada to buy affordable and lifesaving insulin for diabetics like herself. Voting for Quinn is a life or death decision.

Harry Welty wrestles with his conscience and everything else at: lincolndemocrat.com

NOTE: I repeated the title of this column three years later in a series of columns about the trip my wife and I took our grandsons on to see the nation's capital.

The fall of Lincoln (#2)

Thursday Nov. 9th, 2023

The stack of 10,000 Lincoln books found across the street from Ford's Theater. Far below, Welty peers up at the photographer

During a walk from our hotel to the White House, we passed Ford's Theater. We had hoped to see a play there but Ford's wasn't showing summer productions.

In 1971 I had no idea that the infamous site of Lincoln's martyrdom was a functioning theater. Secretary of War, Edwin Stanton, intended to close it permanently. It was confiscated, stripped bare and left a rotting shell. Thus, it remained for decades but it was brought back to life. During my internship I bought tickets to see "You're a good man Charlie Brown." It was an homage to the beloved comic strip "Peanuts" by Minnesota's own Charles Schultz.

My grandsons sat below Lincoln's bunting draped box seats as a National Park ranger told us the theater's history. When they were little the boys gave me a wind-up walking Lincoln much as I gave my grandfather a copy of Bruce Catton's Civil War trilogy. Our family has had many fans of Lincoln. In my grandfather's Era people were proud if they could say, "I shook the hand of man who shook the hand of Lincoln." Having shaken my grandfather's hand, I'm three handshakes from Lincoln.

Lincoln's assassin, actor John Wilkes Booth, had performed for the President and Mrs. Lincoln and had easy access to the theater. He was not the most famous member of his family's acting clan until the murder. After Lincoln was sworn in for a second term Lincoln delivered his 2nd inaugural address calling for malice towards none. Booth, well into his conspiracy, was in the crowd listening. Booth was enraged to hear the proposal to give 300,000 black union soldiers voting rights. He vowed, "That is the last speech will ever make."

Three days later he put his gun to Lincoln's head but too late to stop Southern armies from laying down their weapons. No doubt Booth's spirit was doing cartwheels on January 6th, 2021.

Across from the theater at 516 10th Street stands the Peterson House where Abe breathed his last with son Robert at his side. (Robert Lincoln would also be at the sides of our nation's next two assassinated presidents, James Garfield and William McKinley.) Lincoln's lanky frame was carried by Union soldiers who strained against anxious crowds mobbing the streets as word of the assassination spread. Now a museum its store holds a colossal stack of 10,000 books by different authors devoted to Lincoln's hard to summarize life. I own a dozen myself and just listened on Audible to my newest favorite "Differ we must" by NPR reporter Steve Inskeep.

Another book on my shelves is Doris Kearns Goodwin's "Team of Rivals." It was the template for Steven Spielberg's magnificent film "Lincoln." Kearns Goodwin begins the book by quoting Leo Tolstoy's awestruck praise, "The greatness of Napoleon, Caesar or Washington is only moonlight by the sun of Lincoln.... He was bigger than his country - bigger than all the Presidents together...and as a great character he will live as long as the world lives." Not a bad summary from the man whose War and Peace clocked in at 587,287 words.

I still have the paperback that was my first Lincoln book, "The Day Lincoln was Shot" by Jim Bishop. I read it not long after I complained to my mother that I was ugly. Rather than argue the point Mom simply told me that Abraham Lincoln was a homely man. Lincoln himself famously joked about it. He's been my model ever since.

Lincoln's political career seemed to collapse after his single term in Congress. In 1847 he was out of step with his Illinois voters who were happy with President James Polk's successful war with Mexico. Lincoln saw it as a move to help Democrats at the expense of Whigs by adding slave state territory to United States. And Abe's Whig party all but disappeared as slavery spread. But Lincoln's "ambition," as his law partner James Herndon said, was a little engine that knew no rest." The same could be said of the South which lost the war but which in many ways won the peace by denying newly freed slaves the guarantees of the 13th, 14th and 15th Amendments. And when in 1965 a Democratic president, of all people, restored black voting rights the white South became Republican.

I moved to Minnesota before the magnetic polls switched. Having grown up in Kansas I learned how "Bleeding Kansas" gave birth to the Civil War, the Republican Party and revived the "rail-splitter's" faltering political career. I was deeply chagrined when Minnesota kids started calling me "Reb" because my Kansas accent sounded southern to them. And in my first Minnesota week's I found myself challenged to a wrestling match like Abe when he moved to New Salem.

Every serious American historian has pondered what might have happened if Lincoln had lived. Inskeep's "Differ we must" doesn't go there but it explains how Lincoln dealt with 16 people who strongly disagreed with him over the course of his lifetime. Each episode shows a thoughtfulness all but extinct in the politics of the Fox News Era. It's as though the spirit Tolstoy described had been martyred anew.

Welty keeps Lincoln alive at: www.Lincolndemocrat.com

One of my fellow Kansan's helped push Abe to the sidelines.

Harry Welty's "Bob Dole Singers"

The Ghost of Bob Dole
December 22, 2021

Senator Bob Dole's ghost swept across his home town Russell, Kansas, last Wednesday night. Russell endured record shattering 100 mph winds six days after their native son lay in state in the rotunda of our nation's capitol. While Russell bent to the wind I labored to save a snow sculpture from heavy rains and Minnesota's first ever December tornado watch. I've been thinking a lot about Dole and his similarities to my Grandfather, George Seanor Robb. Both men received well earned praise in death.

Both men were born in rural Kansas. Both enlisted to fight in a World War. My Grandfather fought in WW 1. Bob Dole fought in WW 2. Both got shot to hell. Dole lost the use of his arm. George Robb was awarded the Congressional Medal of Honor. Both men were revered in their respective home towns Russell and Salina. Both went into politics. My grandfather became the Kansas State Auditor for 24 years. Bob Dole was the state's US Senator for 27. The similarities don't end there.

About sixty years ago my grandfather told me that Democrats started all of America's wars. I wrote about this in an Oct. 31, 2002 Reader column: "Never vote for a Democrat and Other Simple Lessons." He told me that the worst mistake of his life was his 1916 presidential vote for Democrat, Woodrow Wilson. Woodrow won by promising to keep American boys out of Europe's First World War." I would have disappointed my Grandfather. While he amassed a 14-1 GOP presidential vote record over 15 elections I could only stomach five Republican presidential votes. I voted for seven Democrats and one Independent - ex-Republican Congressman, John Anderson.

One of my proudest Republican votes was cast in 1976 for President Gerald Ford. I blamed his loss on his Kansas running-mate. Dole repeated my Grandfather's accusation about Democrats starting all the wars on a nationally broadcast debate with Vice President Walter Mondale. Many war veterans were outraged.

My Grandfather died before he could cast his 1972 vote. One week earlier I joined 2,000 Mankato State Students in a peaceful protest march against JFK and LBJ's war. Nixon, a Republican, was the new villain.

Senator Dole died almost a year after his Republican President tried to overthrow the election results on Jan 6th. Until the end Dole supported the "Republican" Trump. This, *I hope*, is where the similarities between Dole and George Robb end.

The Republican Party was different in 1972 the year of the Watergate break-in. There was no Mitch McConnell turning a blind eye to Trump. When push came to shove arch conservative Barry Goldwater, my Grandfather's hero, told President Nixon he had to go.

My Grandfather disliked Franklin Roosevelt and his liberal spending politics but he lived in the era of the "loyal opposition." If anything, the people who later swarmed into Lincoln's *Grand Old Party* were the same people who had always cheated when they were Democrats by denying black Republican voters their voting franchise. Otherwise, my Grandfather bore Democrats no ill will. He saved the jobs of the Democrats in his new office when the Republican Governor who appointed him State Auditor wanted them purged. He liked Harry Truman a veteran who fought just a few miles distant from Grandfather's patch of the Great War. But he still grieved when he learned that his daughter voted with my Dad for Lyndon Johnson in 1964.

I would rather remember Senator Dole as an honest, pragmatic Republican. Suffering war wounds himself he sponsored the big government ADA law for disabled people. During elections he fought Democrats hammer and tong but after the dust settled he worked across the aisles with them. I don't know if Dole had all his marbles when, at age 98, he supported Donald Trump's re-election. I hope he didn't but suspect he did. His wife Elizabeth, also a former US Senator, fired one of her husband's funeral organizers when she learned he had also had a hand in organizing January 6th's treachery.

When I started writing this I couldn't remember if I voted for Dole in 1996 when he ran against Bill Clinton. I did. I found my votes posted on an old website of mine. Bob Dole was the second to last Republican presidential candidate I voted for.

I thought hard about that vote. I even read a short glowing biography of Dole called simply, "Bob Dole," to persuade myself of my vote. I remember reading how he saved himself from one of the right wing's first "primarying" attacks on moderates and how he survived it. He disavowed the Supreme Court's Republican appointee's Roe v. Wade decision. Winning over pro-life votes was a matter of his political survival. It was an early sign of how moderate Republicans would be purged and replaced over the succeeding fifty years to become twenty million strong Trump traitors. That's not such a great legacy.

Up next week: "Why is Michelle Obama in my basement?" NOTE: in this book it's the end of the 9th section.
Everything that Harry writes that is not about the imminent destruction of Earth as we knew it is superfluous. But, he does prattle on at: www.lincolndemocrat.com

JANUARY SIXTH 2021

and making America 2 Again

A Rebel soldier and a blue coat charge each other with bayonets as they are brought back to life by the magical dark arts of the Nation's most divisive President ever.

Paper ballots

Thursday Nov. 3rd, 2022

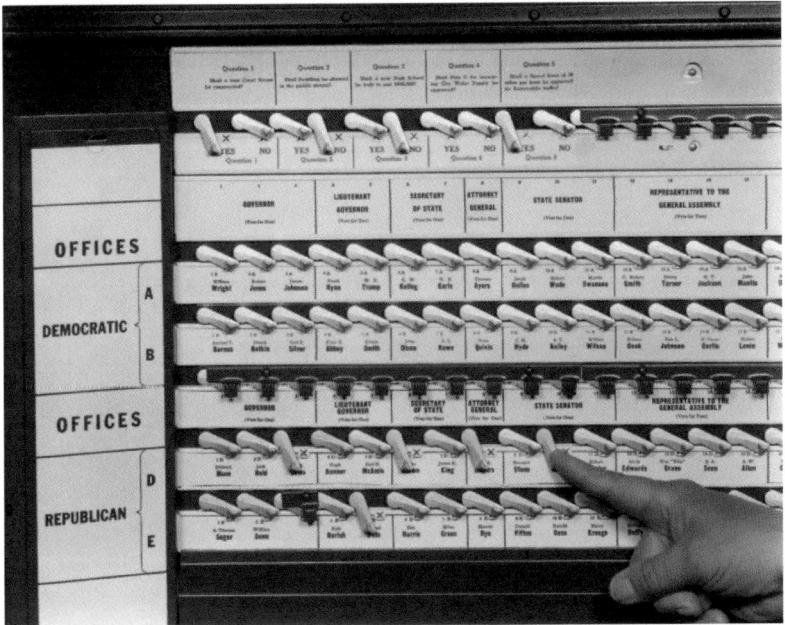

Last week I noted that in 1860 even in the Southern states, where Abe Lincoln was kept off the presidential ballot, no one cried "fraud." No one disputed the election. Angry states simply seceded.

The voting machine was invented in 1881, the same time as states began adopting the secret ballot.

By the time I cast my first ballot in 1972, drawing a curtain around myself like the Wizard of Oz with the pull of a lever, the huge clunky machines were old hat. I'm sure my wife brought our kids in with her behind the curtain to teach them their civic duty by her good example.

Eventually the monster machines gave way to smaller electronic devices that could tally hand filled-out paper ballots. If there were doubts ballots could be counted by hand. Even so, a hand count could be laborious and controversial.

The razor-thin 2000 vote in Florida was short circuited by a Supreme Court majority which briefly forgot its insistence on state election supremacy. This handed Republican candidate George W Bush the presidency and trashed a hand count that would have given the state's electors to Democrat Al Gore.

Gore graciously followed Republican Richard Nixon's 1960 example and conceded the election.

In 1960 pre-South Republicans thought the thin democratic victories in Illinois and Texas had a funny smell. Southern Democrats were the most proficient election riggers in America.

For a century after the passage of the 15th Amendment Southern Democrats insured that few if any slave descendants were allowed to vote. All those uncast votes were reliably Republican.

I was 14 before that changed with the passage of the Voting Rights Act. Surprise, surprise! Not long afterwards southern Dems switched partners and gradually the Party of Lincoln was itching to gut the Voting Rights Act. Then it came to pass with a Republicanized Supreme Court.

This didn't prevent Joe Biden from getting elected so someone's partisans attempted Jan 6, 2021, overthrow.

Now Republicans are demanding a return to paper ballots. Internet rumors tell us that remote malefactors are changing votes inside voting machines. Gun-toting Republicans are confident they can mosey over to voters, drop boxes and ballot counters all will be well so long as votes are cast on paper. Never mind that Florida's infamous hanging chads were all on paper ballots.

In the early 2000s I wanted to prove to fetus-loving Republicans that I, too, remembered Democratic shenanigans. I was going to write a tell-all about the 1978 election when scandals helped Republicans rout the DFL in the "Minnesota

Massacre."

Despite a couple years' research I was never up to explaining such a convoluted tale but that search led me to an even earlier episode of DFL chicanery from 1962. That was the year before I moved to Minnesota.

Senator Hubert H. Humphrey, a DFL hero, cooked up a fake highway contracting scandal that cost squeaky clean Republican Governor Elmer Andersen dearly while he was running for reelection.

Even so, a first recount declared Andersen the winner by a threadbare 142-vote margin. More recounts ensued. The 500,000 machine-cast ballots were never questioned but the 800,000 paper ballots were. They got counted over and over. By January 97,000 votes were challenged, a huge number. This was whittled down to 3,851 suspect ballots. In them lay victory or defeat.

In my book research phase I inter-viewed a one-time DFL contender for Governor. He told me what one of the DFL attorneys participating in the 1963 recount told him. The attorney palmed a pencil as he thumbed through ballots. He surreptitiously marked irksome ballots in such a way that a later vote counter might consider them spoiled in further recounts.

On March 25, 139 days after the November election, Democrat Karl Rolvaag was sworn in as Governor, having won by 91 votes. That was just a hair more than one vote per Minnesota's 87 counties.

I moved to Duluth in 1974, intent on becoming a missionary for good government Republicanism. My antennae were up. My college Republican friends had joked about the communist gun range in Cherry, Minnesota. The Iron Range is where many a Republican campaign went to die.

In only slightly less Democratic Duluth, as everywhere else, Minnesota law required that both major parties have equal numbers of election judges and poll watchers during elections. The problem was that there were hardly any Republicans in a lot of precincts.

You really couldn't hold up an election because one party was unable to field election monitors, so a blind eye was turned and many Democrats become honorary elephants on election day. These were honest people a little embarrassed by their white lies, but Democrats won such lopsided victories there was no cause for mischief.

But today with partisanship taking on cult-like power I can't help but think of that pencil-palming lawyer when I watch Trump's attorneys make their cases for a President who refused to say he'd abide by the election results and in fact who had been plotting for six months before the election to call it a fraud and sabotage it.

Harry Welty also shoots off his mouth at lincolndemocrat.com.

My Kind of Loser
August 30, 2018

Caucus McCain 2000

This is the header of the website that Harry Welty used for John McCain's 2000 presidential campaign.

My Republican grandfather had a soft spot for Arizona Senator Barry Goldwater. When, after the 1964 presidential election, he learned that his daughter (my mother) had voted for a Democrat, Lyndon Johnson, it almost broke his heart. That election put conservatism out to pasture for the rest of the decade and made Goldwater a byword for loser among the young, liberal, JFK worshiping crowd I went to college with.

In 1971 I got an opportunity to spend the summer in Congress as a college intern for a good-natured Republican Congressman, Ancher Nelsen. He was so reviled for being a Republican that no one from the neighboring college, Gustavus Adolphus, was willing to work for him that summer. That was good fortune for me as I was about to become a sophomore at Mankato State College. It gave me the opportunity to attend lectures by some of the leading lights of the 1970's.

At the time my political hero was one of the last Republican liberals, Senator John Percy of Illinois. I eagerly attended a lecture he gave to an auditorium full of college interns. Although I didn't know it Senator Percy had a hearing aid. When he kept asking students to repeat their questions some of them began to let loose loud histrionic sighs of disbelief and impatience. For these rude, young progressives Percy, liberal as he was, was a detested Republican. His hearing disability only served to inflame and stiffen their condescension.

If John Percy received a rude greeting from my intern peers I hate to think about the welcome they gave my Grandfather's hero, Barry Goldwater. I did not witness it because, like my parents, I was not a fan of his. Nonetheless, despite Goldwater's defense of American involvement in Vietnam and skepticism of the civil rights movement I felt he was owed respect. When I later heard how raucously he had been treated by my fellow interns I was incensed. These self-righteous young jerks might just as well have insulted my Grandfather as far as I was concerned. This episode helped coax me into the arms of the College Republican as the 1972 presidential election gathered steam. I still had no intention of voting for Richard Nixon. My candidate was the ex-marine and anti-war Congressman Pete McCloskey who got a single vote for President at the Republican National Convention in Miami. Much to his chagrin, it deprived Richard Nixon of a unanimous vote.

On Saturday a second, conservative, Arizona Senator "loser," John McCain, died. Even in death McCain was treated with more disrespect than his predecessor Goldwater was treated by those liberal college kids back in 1971. However, the rude treatment heaped on the departed McCain came at the hands of the sitting "Republican" President of the United States. I'll never forgive the draft dodging Trump for calling McCain a loser because the young aviator was caught, imprisoned and tortured by the Vietnamese. Compare Trump to Pham Minh Chuc, one of McCain's torturers, who showered his former prisoner with accolades upon hearing of the Senator's death.

Unlike McCain's predecessor Goldwater, I stood one hundred percent behind McCain in the 2000 Presidential election. That was the year that "Deep State" big money Republicans sabotaged McCain ahead of the racially sensitive South Carolina primary by robo-calling Republican voters to tell them that McCain had fathered a black daughter. Later that year the newly Republicanized Supreme Court took away the decision to rule on the results of Florida's presidential vote from Florida's courts to insure a Republican Presidency rather than one lead by Vice President Al Gore, a Democrat.

It's been hard for me to sympathize with self-righteous Republicans since that election even though I think I cast a reluctant vote for Bush. I took that election to heart because I was effectively the head of the Duluth for McCain campaign. As such, I put a website up for McCain as well as a homemade four-by-eight-foot lawnsign in my yard.

What the Republican Party did to John McCain helps explain how it managed to make Donald Trump's snake oil look more honest to the latest iteration of the "Republican base." If the Party of Lincoln is to survive Trumpism it must somehow rediscover the soul of the second Arizona Senator to be called a loser and hope that it rises again from the ashes like the bird for which Arizona's capital takes its name.

Harry Welty is a local eccentric, and "perennial candidate," who also pontificates on his blog: www.lincolndemocrat.com

Smaller than a Bread Basket
Published July 21, 2005

Although most Minnesotans have never heard of him or the organization he is President of (Americans for Tax Reform) Grover Norquist seems to have single-handedly disqualified Minnesota Governor Tim Pawlenty, from consideration as a potential presidential nominee of the Republican Party in 2008. While plenty of Minnesotans would not find this very alarming the man who exercises such power is worth examining.

Grover Norquist's passion, tax reduction, represents one of the more secular impulses of the Republican Party. Like the internationally interventionist neo-cons and the gun doting NRA types (whose Board Norquist sits on) his interests are less theological than those of the religious 'conservatives' whose little engine drives the Party.

Just how secular was inadvertently demonstrated a week ago in his reply to a survey by the staff of the New Republic. The TNR Online asked two-dozen leading conservative thinkers what they thought of the chief bugaboo of the religious right, evolution. A breathtaking sample of these conservatives believed in evolution although for his part Grover Norquist's response suggested indifference to the subject. But a throwaway line of Grover's, which the TNR quoted, was eye popping.

Where evolution was concerned, said Norquist, "The problem here is that you shouldn't have government run schools. Given that we (Americans for Tax Reform) have to spend all our time crushing the capital gains tax I don't have much time for this issue."

Well, thank goodness! Grover is too busy preserving the mammon of America's richest political contributors and can't afford to divert his attention to shutting down public schools. ("Mammon," by the way, is the Bible's pejorative for ungodly wealth.) It's not enough that *Americans for Tax Reform* has already dealt a deathblow to the Estate Tax. Grover and company won't be satisfied until all taxes are stamped out. After that he will he turn his attention to public education.

Norquist's pet name for government is the "beast" which also happens to be what Revelations, the fire-and-brimstone last book of the Bible, calls Satan. Norquist's mission is nothing less than to shrink government down to the size of a breadbasket. Perhaps it should come as no surprise that he has found common cause with religious conservatives.

Norquist's distaste for the beast puts him just a peg above anarchists who believe that government is the only thing that stands in the way of utopia. It's surprising the number of people who hold similar views. Marxist/Leninists regard government as a temporary condition on the way to the Worker's Paradise and fundamentalists expect "the elect" to rapture right out of their clothes directly to heaven as the corrupt reign of man on Earth is brought to a fiery end.

Governor Pawlenty's crime was to have violated a pledge not to raise taxes by proposing a 75 cent-a-pack tax boost on cigarettes. Why, only the week before Norquist's organization had hailed the Governor as a "Hero of the Taxpayer."

Americans for Tax Reform must have been sorely disappointed in their fallen "hero" once reality kicked in.

From the moment Minnesota Democrats swept so many Republicans legislators out of office in the 2004 elections it was inevitable that Pawlenty would have to compromise on his tax pledge. Like his allies the Biblical literalists Norquist is a true believer and has little patience for that dirty political word: compromise.

Putting an end to the teaching of evolution in government-run schools may be down Grover Norquist's list of priorities but once he and his allies get rid of public education government really will be smaller than a breadbasket. It will be more like an amoeba. Now that really is de-evolution.

Welty is a small time politician who lets it all hang out at: *www.snowbizz.com*

The Night That Donald Trump was Elected President
Published Oct. 8 2020

"Our surprise house guest on election night 2016"

(last Friday night, thirty days before the 2020 Presidential election, Donald Trump was put on oxygen and admitted to Walter Reed Hospital for a disease that kills one in every 33 people it infects. It prompted this memory)

The night Donald Trump was elected President of the United States I wrote in my blog, "America is like the character Dustin Hoffman played in the Graduate after he raced off from the church with his runaway bride and sat panting on the bus wondering what the hell he'd just done."

On election night 2016 I was in my childhood home Topeka, Kansas. It's the only election night I have not spent with my wife Claudia. She had to watch the results without anyone to console her. I was on a mission to honor my maternal grandfather, George Seanor Robb.

I had been invited by the American Legion Post he once belonged to. They had rediscovered that one of their own had been the recipient of the nation's highest military award the Congressional Medal of Honor. They were inscribing his name in a place of honor and wanted a family representative with them on the 98th anniversary of World War I's Armistice. The ceremony would fall two days after a Presidential election that all the pundits guaranteed would pave the way for our first pantsuit wearing President.

I was not so sanguine. A few days before I left I had put up my fourth anti-Trump lawn decoration since his demagogic campaign had begun. It was a hastily drawn sign reading "Manchurian Candidate" with a vivid red diagonal slash.

I was using the trip to research my Grandfather's life at his Alma Mater and at the Kansas State Historical Museum where my Mother had placed his correspondence.

After some initial research at Park College near Kansas City, Missouri, I drove to Topeka's Ramada Inn on Election day. It was jumping with a rapturous crowd anticipating the election of our first female President. I crossed my fingers for them. Like some animals I sometimes feel the tremors of an earthquake before the Earth splits open.

Sometime after Trump's shock and awe was beyond doubt I ventured down to the lobby and found stunned and mute silence. I spent the following day and the next at the Historical Society photographing the letters of a Kansas war hero turned Republican State Auditor. I hoped to write a book about a very brave and honorable man.

My most satisfying discovery was a letter George Robb had written to the President of Park College upon learning that he was disinclined to enroll a Japanese-American student during the heat of the Second World War. There is little doubt that this young man's family was languishing behind the barbed wire of an "internment" camp. In the strongest words the Kansas State Auditor and war hero urged the boy's admission. It was in keeping with his Republican character. Twenty-three years earlier my Grandfather, a white officer, had been assigned to an all-black American Infantry division recruited in New York's Harlem.

My Grandfather's Republican Party was different then; fiercely loyal to the memory of its paragon, Abraham Lincoln. Grandfather told me that his worst mistake in life was voting for a Democrat, Woodrow Wilson for President. He warned me not to follow his example. He voted for the Democrat because of Wilson's promise to keep America out of Europe's War. Despite Wilson's betrayal, George Robb was one of the first to volunteer when war was declared. His credo? "My country right or wrong." And yet my Grandfather bore Democrats no ill will. He defied Republican Governor Alf Landon's order to fire the Democrats in the Auditor's Office. He told my Mother that he liked the Democratic President Harry S.Truman.

As I write this America is waiting to see if President Trump will emerge from his hospitalization and return to the campaign trail from the infection he brought to Duluth last week. Unlike the President, Democrat Joe Biden has followed an example my Grandfather would expect. Joe called for prayers for the President. Biden dropped in on Duluth just ahead of Mr. Trump's visit and was filmed walking over to a small crowd of Trump supporters waving their candidate's signs. Joe shook their hands.

The morning after the 2016 election Claudia sent me a photograph she took on election night looking down from our patio. A black bear was climbing the stairs after triggering our burglar lights. Perhaps he was an emissary from Putin's Internet trolling Russia checking on our Anti-Manchurian Candidate sign. I'm sorry Grandfather. It's not easy to be magnanimous these days but just maybe Joe Biden, a Democrat, is a harbinger of a return to a "more perfect union."

Harry Welty encourages his eight loyal readers to read the speech he gave on November 12th, 2016 at his blog: www.lincolndemocrat.com

Purging the RINOs

Thursday Jan. 14th, 2021

A logo Harry drew a quarter century ago to advertise his unwillingness to march lock step with the the brain dead.

I watched my television slack jawed all day at an attempted overthrow of American Government. I hadn't spent a day like that since 9/11. One Trump supporter echoed Timothy McVeigh's bible the Turner Diaries. He told an NPR reporter he wanted to set up gallows and hang our congressman four by four at a time for their treachery. Donald Trump had exhorted them to get Pence too. He would be with them on their rampage.......in spirit evidently. Trump stayed back at the White House almost giddy, like the Sorcerer's Apprentice, but surprised that others there didn't seem to share his delight. When they broke into the Capitol the Trumplicans carried the Confederate Stars and Bars. That's the flag of Lincoln's assassin, John Wilkes Booth.

Purging the RINOS

After five years of describing Donald Trump as a demagogue the cornered President fully vindicated my fears. His storm troopers put Black Lives Matter protesters to shame in the capitol that was built with slave labor before the Civil War. I saw baby strollers being pushed at the edge of the crowd. It was like a Southern necktie party with families bringing picnic baskets to show their children a lynching.

Forty percent of Republicans still support Trump unequivocally. That's enough to scare the bejesus out of the elected Republicans who will face primaries in two more years.

Up to now these pols have given Trump cover for all of his lies including the outrageous claim that he won the election. But those who joined democrats to validate an honest election were simply the latest crop of the Republican Party's most detested traitors - RINOs. (Republicans in Name Only)

It's not Lincoln's Party. It's not Reagan's Party. It's Trump's party now. That became obvious at the 2016 Republican National convention when Trump threatened to leave and take his delegates with him like the Dixiecrats did at the Democratic Convention in 1948. They left because Truman integrated "Negroes" into the Armed Forces. And that's why seeing the Confederate Stars and Bars was so appropriate. Its a party John Wilkes Booth would join. Trump's people don't consider themselves Republicans.

It is odd to hear the sometimes Democrat, sometimes pro-choice opportunist, Trump, call Pence and his ilk RINO's. One good turncoat deserves another. Republicans have been doing this since "Big Tent" Ronald Reagan got Alzheimer's. Now its Trump's loyal Vice President Pence's turn with a bonus - death threats. On the eve of the vote to accept the electoral college Trump reportedly told Pence "I don't want to be your friend anymore." Poor Mike reminds me of the dogs under the feet of marble kings sculpted on Gothic sarcophagi where they were laid to rest.

By 1980's the South's Dixiecrats were fully integrated into the once hated "Party of Lincoln." Reagan announced his candidacy in Alabama just miles from the infamous site where three young freedom fighters were murdered for registering black voters. Back then every week some Democratic politician publicly switched parties to become a Republican. Then Republicans began calling the democratic party the "Democrat" Party. God forbid anyone call them democratic! Evidently only Republicans were democratic. To prove it they incorporated the old southern strategy of making it hard for black citizens to vote. They had a new Republican Supreme Court to help them and they wanted even more Republicans on the Court. Is it any surprise that the people who stormed the Capitol were almost all white?

I understand why the Republican congressmen who had to take shelter during the attack are reluctant to declare support for Trump's impeachment. It used to be their offices they were afraid of losing. Now its their lives.

Of all the images I saw the one that reminded me how far the Republican party has fallen was the pot bellied protester who climbed up on President Gerald Ford's pedestal in Statuary Hall. He had stuck one of Trump's billowing blue snot rags in the crook of Ford's bronzed elbow. Jerry would have looked happier with pigeon droppings.

The natural world is down to two white rhinoceroses today. When they die it will be the last we see of one of natures marvels. But the ever self-purging Republican party has grown a new crop of RINOs. Those are the Republicans who won't lick Donald Trump's boots. In my childhood democrats didn't worry about marrying republicans. No more. Nowadays they'd have to kiss them.

Harry Welty evades extinction and anonymity at: www.lincolndemocrat.com

The Rich men north of Richmond Debate

Wed. Jan. 12th, 2022

 After the Fox presidential debate my wife texted her brother in law: *"Last night I was watching Breaking Bad on the second floor; Harry was watching the debate on the first floor; and the boys were watching Bodies, Bodies, Bodies in the basement. We aren't sure which of us had the scariest viewing.*

 As a beleaguered fan of democracy I warily watched Fox's Presidential debate. It began with the unbalanced assertions of GOP Wisconsinites who unanimously explained that despite the lowest unemployment levels since my infancy seventy years ago Biden was ruining America's economy. To frame the debate Fox, which is desperately sucking up to Trumpers, proceeded to play a little of the Oliver Anthony music video that is taking Red America by storm, **"Rich men north of Richmond"**

It may not have occurred to Fox that the candidate who was boycotting their debate, *the elephant who wasn't in the room,* is a *rich man North of Richmond* who visited the "minors" on Jeffrey Epstein's tropical island. If I was a Trump fan that song would make me queasy. And to add insult to ignorance Oliver's anthem trashes 300 pound welfare people. All that diabetes killing weight comes from eating corn syrup grown in Trump subsidized Republican farm country.

I saw a lot more sucking up to Trump in Milwaukee than I saw in 2016 when Republicans couldn't believe how Trump was plowing them under. I also noticed some Trump fatigue when candidates suggesting the party could do better than Trump got some respectable cheers. But the audience kept the candidates on a short leash. Chris Christie was showered with boos when he accused Trump of running on a revenge platform but he pressed on to say that Trump's actions were unbecoming of a president of the United States. Thirty-eight year old entrepreneur, Vivek Rammaswami, sprang to 45's defense winning cheers as he accused Christie of his own revenge campaign against Trump.

The most awkward appearance was Vice President Pence still haunted by the spectre of a hangman's noose. He pointedly asked the other candidates if they agreed he was right to defend the Constitution over Donald Trump. The others all reluctantly agreed that he had done the right thing but the young Trump impersonator, Ramaswammi, quickly added that if elected he would pardon Trump.

When the debate hosts asked the eight to raise their hands if they planned to support Trump if he got the nomination only Arkansas Governor Asa Hutchinson's hand remained at his side. Their timidity follows Trump's take over of a party after fifty years of repeated purges of independent minded Republicans.

Goldwaterites chased out Rockefeller liberals. Nixonites froze out anti-war Republicans. Reaganites hounded anyone who didn't go along with what George HW Bush called "voodoo economics." Bush saved himself by becoming pro-life thereby abandoning a lot of people like my parents who were pro-choice. Those who thought some regulation of big business was prudent were sidelined by the deep pockets of the Republican party's Deep State. Worship of promiscuous gun ownership; neutering the audits of the rich by the Internal Revenue Service and shelving Civil Rights only added to the refugees.

By 2016 so much purification had taken place that the canny, one-time New York liberal, Donald Trump, did a 180 and took up the banner of geriatric skirt chasing Bible thumpers and blue collar workers whose unions had been dismembered by the "right to work" Republican Party. Trump himself had been quick to churn out cheep ties in China.

And that brings me back to the lyrics of Debate night's theme song.

It describes how the Donald Trumps of America left the poor behind. Those rich include Donald Trump's son in law Jared who, six months after Trump's fingers were pried of the door jambs of the White House, made a cool 2 billion from the same Saudis who butchered a Washington Post Reporter and put his body parts in their carry-on luggage. Or the billionaires who have saved a jaw dropping 2 trillion dollars each year in tax cuts from the Republican's 2017 tax cuts.

Democrats should steal Oliver Anthony's battle cry the way Bill Clinton stole NAFTA from the Republicans to prepare for the looming battle of our soon-to-be octogenarians. As I said before, unemployment under Joe is the lowest its been since I was in diapers.

I leave you some of Oliver Anthony's pertinent lyrics. Decide for yourself which party they are more suited to:

Rich Men North Of Richmond" Oliver Anthony

It's a damn shame what the world's gotten to
For people like me and people like you
Wish I could just wake up and it not be true
But it is, oh, it is

Livin' in the new world
With an old soul
These rich men north of Richmond
Lord knows they all just wanna have total control
Wanna know what you think, wanna know what you do
And they don't think you know, but I know that you do
'Cause your dollar ain't shit and it's taxed to no end
'Cause of rich men north of Richmond

Harry Welty will try to keep the Reader's editor happy by meeting his deadlines.........until he can't.

I WAS A BROWN BABY
1950-1963

("Brown" as in *Linda Brown vs. Topeka Board of Education*. My parents moved into a Topeka home where they knew I would soon be part of an integrated elementary school. NOTE:the image above is Ruby Bridges not Linda Brown)

The Topeka's Schools obeyed the Supreme Court

This class photo was taken in 1962 when I was in sixth grade. It was my last year in Kansas before we moved to North Mankato, Minnesota. Loman Hill Elementary began integrating

113

in 1955 the year following the Supreme Court's Brown v. Topeka Board of Education decision. I have two class pictures from second grade. The first was taken in November before the new children from segregated Buchanan Elementary were transferred to Loman Hill. It shows 21 white kids, 2 Asian kids, and 3 African-American kids. In a March photograph there is one fewer Asian child and 5 more white kids. There are also two additional black kids in the picture. Over the next several years the proportions of kids in my class changed. By sixth grade there were 14 white kids and 18 minority kids, including Sammy an Osage Indian, in Mr. Ross's class.

God Made Us That Way
Published Dec 26, 2002

When I was about six years old I embarrassed my mother while we rode home on a Topeka city bus. We sat next to a black woman we did not know, and I piped up "Why are you that color?"

"Because God made me that way," she patiently explained.

This was about the time that a Moses-like Strom Thurmond began leading a southern exodus from the Democratic Party to The Promised Land - the once hated "Party of Lincoln." Oh, but God works in mysterious ways.

Kansas had been a "free" state during Lincoln's "War of Northern Aggression." Unfortunately, despite the state's early liberality its Capitol, Topeka, had set up "separate but equal" public schools just like those in Thurmond's South Carolina. The Supreme Court put an end to this in 1954 with Brown vs. Topeka Board of Education.

Not long after the Brown decision, at the beginning of my second-grade year, I climbed up and sat atop the jungle gym during recess. From my perch I watched colored children from the segregated Buchanan Elementary School file into my school, Loman Hill. Each black child had walked the five or so blocks holding their chairs in front of them with text books neatly stacked on the seats. The youngest children led the procession. When they reached our school they were sorted by grade into their new classrooms which were also our new classrooms. Topeka gave in easily. Strom Thurmond did not.

Sometime during these years my grandfather made a prediction. He told my mother that America would eventually become a nation of brown people. That claim would have sent Thurmond into a frenzy. Strom railed tirelessly against "race mixing" and he wasn't just complaining about school integration. Strom was talking about the "mongrelization" of the white race.

To prevent mongrelization from occurring Southern states had passed "anti-miscegenation" laws. This was one of the first 50 cent words I ever learned. I discovered it in one of the subversive magazines of the day, Life, Look, or the Saturday Evening Post. It was in a sensational article about a white man who had been imprisoned for the crime of marrying a black woman. If state's rights could only prevail over the Supreme Court then southern states could use their statutory law as a shield to ward off my grandfather's dire prediction.

Grandfather was a learned man who had come to have a low regard for Thomas Jefferson. I have never been sure why he felt this way about the author of the Declaration of Independence but I have a theory. I think Grandfather suspected that Jefferson had sired children by his deceased wife's half sister and slave, Sally Hemmings. Although many historians once dismissed this allegation recent DNA evidence has convinced most that this was indeed the case. DNA evidence wasn't available to my grandfather. The only things available to him were his knowledge of history and human nature.

Despite Jefferson's unwillingness to free his own slaves and his hypocrisy he had already sown the seeds that would kill the institution of slavery. Four score and seven years later Abraham Lincoln took Jefferson's words and replanted them in the blood soaked ground of Gettysburg. He told us about "a new birth of freedom" for a nation, "under God," "dedicated to the proposition that all men are created equal." (I can't help but wonder if Strom ever gave this much thought as he marched his people to the Republican Promised Land?)

Strom may have one more thing in common with Thomas Jefferson - a more carnal hand in bringing about grandfather's prediction. You see, Thurmond is widely believed to have fathered the light skinned daughter of a black, teenage, housemaid who worked in his home. He was a school superintendent at the time of this child's birth. Although she denies that Strom is her father, Thurmond has apparently supported the woman financially all her life. He even made sure that she received a college education. So far no one has pushed for a DNA test but the circumstantial evidence is compelling. If the story is true there is one more small irony. The man who fought ferociously against miscegenation would no longer be charged with that crime. Of course, in today's world he might have to face charges of statutory rape.

At one hundred Strom doesn't have many years left to wrestle with his conscience. As for the rest of us, well, we would all be well advised to remember that our adversaries today may someday be the ancestors of our own descendants.

It's been suggested that "racism is as American as apple pie." So apparently are illicit sex and hypocrisy. How strange it is to think that these sorry conditions have, in their own circuitous way, helped bring us all together. Could that be what God had in mind?

Harry Welty is a small time politician who lets it all hang out at www.snowbizz.com

The MP who pulled black men off white prostitutes – The rest of the Story.

Note: This is is modified from a blog post of the same date as my column titled: "**Kicking the 'N' word out of ISD 709.**" The post added context for this paragraph in my column:

"I heard the "N" word precious few times when I was attending a newly integrated elementary school. We knew better and I was shocked when my kindergarten neighbor told me she didn't want to go to school with "no niggers." This was not a terribly surprising attitude for a six-year-old considering that her Father had been required to pull black soldiers off white prostitutes in Italy's Red-Light Districts after World War II."

Walt deserves better than I gave him. Walt was the MP that pulled black men off Italian prostitutes. The operative word here is *"white"* prostitutes.

I was wary of Walt when I first laid eyes on him as a little kid. Getting a real kick out of him would take time. It didn't hurt that he once took me fishing at the pretty little stream near Lake Wabaunsee. Perhaps he took me along because he no longer had a son to fish with.

Our families moved in next to each other just before I started second grade. Walt bought the house my mother had grown up in and our family moved into the tiny house next door that her Aunt Verna once occupied. Getting used to Walt took some doing. I sized him up while he leaned on the fence between our houses, chomped on a cigar and talked to my dad.

Walt and his wife had two daughters. The little one was the kindergartner mentioned in my column. Her older sister would later babysit for me and my siblings. The family used to have a son but he was electrocuted after a rainstorm by poorly maintained overhead lines. The grieving parents took the powerful Kansas Power and Light to court and discovered how vicious and stingy a big company can be in excusing its mistakes. The KPL attorneys accused Walt and his wife of trading on their son's death to make a quick buck. That's what my mother told me. Mom and Joyce became very close friends.

I can picture Walt as a military policeman. I wouldn't have wanted to tangle with him. He swore, he spit and he smoked cigars. One evening when I was within earshot of Walt's front porch I told another kid about the tough guy next door. I said Walt swore, spat and smoked cigars. Of course, Walt's oldest daughter overheard me and indignantly told her dad what the rotten little kid next door had said about him. Walt thought it was the funniest damned thing he'd ever heard.

For years after leaving Topeka, on our returns we'd pay a call on Walt's family and at every visit Walt would retell that story. Every time he'd get to *'he swears, he spits and he smokes cigars'* Walt would bust a gut in delight.

In Italy, Walt was just doing what he was ordered to do by his superior officers. It would have been unpleasant no matter the race of the GI's caught in the sweep of a brothel. I know how racist our military was, especially among its southern officers. It wouldn't be integrated for another three years after World War II. Officers did everything in their power to prevent black soldiers from fighting lest they earn respect, glory or medals. American officers were scandalized that European women didn't know better than to fraternize with black men.

This was true in the First World War as well where my white grandfather officer-ed the Harlem Hellfighters, black soldiers from New York. The 369th infantry had an unusual birth. White Republicans fought for years to get a black infantry unit started and when war was declared they got their wish. They became its officers. My Kansas grandfather was assigned to the unit which, because American officers generally wanted nothing to do with black men, was attached to the French Fourth Army.

Whatever racial prejudices Walt, the Kansas boy, took to World War II his service in Italy only served to reinforce them. Brown vs. Board of Education didn't help. The school I was about to attend with Walt's children had just been integrated by the United States Supreme Court. In the five years I attended it Loman Hill Elementary took in more and more black children. After my family left for Minnesota a black principal was assigned to the school. To say that white parents were unhappy is a considerable understatement. We all wondered how Walt would take this given his history. We got a pleasant surprise.

Walt became a leader of the parents and worked with principal to make his transition a smooth one. That's it. The end of the story. Walt became a hero. The world can become a better place.

Perhaps we shouldn't have been so surprised. There was that night during the Cuban Missile Crisis that my mother had a nightmare about Fidel Castro stuffing people in a bag. She was so frozen in terror that she couldn't move even though she knew she had to warn the people in her dream. She screwed up her courage and let out a scream so loud it blasted through her open autumn window and woke the whole neighborhood.

Across our fence Walt the old MP shot up, scrambled out of bed, fetched his rifle and began patrolling our neighborhood. My mom rolled over and went back to sleep never confessing her part in the drama. As for Walt. He just did what you would have expected from a tough guy who swore, who spat, and who smoked cigars.

Everything Harry writes that is not about the imminent destruction of Earth as we knew it is superfluous. But, he does prattle on at www.lincolndemocrat.com.

NO PAPER BAGS

NOTE: The bag is explained in the dedication of this book.

Hearts Behind Bars
Published July12, 2002

When my son and daughter were little they learned how to play hearts at Duluth's Federal Prison. For about a year our family made monthly visits to Dave, a close friend of my wife's sister and her husband. He had been convicted of embezzling $75,000 from his employer's credit union. Dave and his wife were DINKS. (Double Income, No Kids) They lived in a nice house on a lake but apparently Dave didn't think they had enough to keep up with the Jones's.

We got to see an interesting collection of humanity in the prison's visiting room. The inmates were roughly divided into two groups - Black drug pushers and White white collar criminals. We were mostly introduced to white inmates and their visitors like the bitter woman whose husband took the fall when her friend ratted on her for dumping heavy metal residues from their business into Lake Michigan. She didn't much care for the EPA.

Dave wryly pointed out the mutual disdain white and black inmates held for each other. White embezzlers, he explained, looked down on the black prisoners because of their unwholesome commodity. Black drug dealers looked down on the white collar criminals for taking what didn't belong to them. White thieves were proud that they hadn't poisoned anyone. Black inmates were proud to have offered their customers a service while partaking in that most American of activities: commerce.

Commerce has been on my mind lately what with all the news stories about Enron, Arthur Anderson, Global Crossings, etc. It's reminded me of all those games of hearts we played among the felons whose commercial ventures caught up with them. The simple motivation behind every one of those inmates was greed. It's the same motivation behind all the current news headlines in the business world and it's a big deal. The headlines are shaking the nation's confidence in the stock market and threatening the economy. There's a lot of finger pointing going on in Washington over who to blame. There is a very fine line between commerce and larceny. It's called ethics.

I got my lesson in ethics from my folks. In fact, politics, money and my dad's ethics are what landed my family in Minnesota. When my dad was a kid in Independence, Missouri, he was offended by Boss Pendergast's corrupt Democratic machine in neighboring Kansas City. All those corrupt Democrats turned my dad into a Republican. Even some Pendergast's cronies, like Harry Truman, were embarrassed by the machine's reputation. After he got elected to the U.S. Senate Harry jumped at the chance to spruce up his reputation. He did it, just like today's congressman, by chairing a Senate Committee investigating war profiteering.

After my dad was admitted to the bar he worked for the Kansas State Insurance Commission. He prided himself on keeping unscrupulous insurance companies out of the state. He had hopes of advancing in office until he made the mistake of advising his boss not to accept gifts from the companies they regulated. After a more circumspect colleague won the promotion that my dad had wanted he realized he'd better move on. We packed our bags and moved to Minnesota and he started teaching law at Mankato State .

I entertained some hope for Dave's redemption but I'm sorry to report that during his stay I never got the sense that Dave ever realized he was a crook. As far as he was concerned his was just a matter of bad timing. (I've been hearing much the same excuse from the halls of corporate America lately) If Dave had just had a little more time he would have paid everything back and no one would have been any the wiser.

Dave couldn't hide his admiration (or maybe it was envy) for an even bigger embezzler. The object of his admiration was a Twin City's banker who had absconded with several millions of dollars, a sum which dwarfed Dave's take. Like Dave, this fellow had persuaded himself that if only he'd been given a little more time everything would have worked out. This bigger chiseler received many supportive friends during our visits. After he was released they saw to it that a good job was waiting for him although he wasn't happy with the measly $120,000 salary it offered.

The drug dealers haven't got it all wrong. Commerce is the lifeblood of the nation and in the next few years the drug dealers can expect to meet many representatives of the business world as they head to Duluth to serve their prison terms. It will keep the courts and the politicians busy for some time to come. In the meantime, my kids still know how to play hearts.

A friend told me that she thought my last column pooh poohed Tim Penny's chances of winning the Governorship. Au contraire! I was probably just too oblique to get my point across, to wit: If Jesse couldn't win four years ago Tim can't win today. In other words – Don't take the predictions that Penny can't win this year any more seriously than the predictions about Jesse losing four years ago. And the odds for Penny have improved now that he's chosen a popular Republican State Senator to be his running mate. If the Republicans hadn't denied Martha Robertson the Senate endorsement because she was pro choice, Penny wouldn't have been able to add her to his arsenal.

Welty is a small time politician who lets it all hang out at: www.snowbizz.com

A Campaign Flyer

I have been a cross for my family to bear from the beginning of my entry into politics. My wife never made the pledge to honor me in sickness and health but she has put up with a lot ever since I picked her up in a bar. *Haw, Haw!* She hates the way I told that story to my Church's men's group

For my children who attended the school system, the Board of which I finally got myself elected to, it was even more challenging. They were just kids. Above you see the only family photo I used in a campaign brochure. Its wonderful and I used it again on that year's Christmas letter. See my engaging son. He hated being in that picture but by golly he smiled the most winning smile ever for his deluded father.

Now my son's almost 40. He has secured a place in life a thousand miles away where his last name may not be connected to his father's political antics. I couldn't completely resist mentioning him on my website, blog or in my Duluth Reader columns. My daughter who still lives in town took her husband's name so she has a little cover. She has the thicker skin of an extrovert.

I've always been sympathetic to the families whose politician father, son, aunt or namesake gets in the news. You can see it in the drug recovering Hunter Biden and Donald Trump's son-in-law Jared who secured a 2 billion dollar deal from the king who had a Washington Post reporter sawed into cutlets for his carry-on-luggage.

In the bag
Thursday Sep. 16th, 2021

Keely Welty *not* wearing a paper bag.

Jesus was in the Wilderness 40 days. Churchill was in his between World Wars, 1 and 2. I've been there twice.
The most significant was my estrangement from the Party of Lincoln in 1992. Before that I wandered the wilderness after losing my third teaching job in 1987. That lasted until I was

finally elected to the school board in 1994.

My first wilderness experience coincided with my daughter starting first grade and my becoming a house dad. We had just moved to 21st Avenue East. Without a job I was keen to fulfill her request: "Daddy, make me a snow dinosaur."

Cunning man that I am I decided snow sculpting might help make my rehabilitation possible. A few months earlier I had told my father on his death bed that despite having lost three teaching jobs I was thinking of running for the school board. The look in his eyes and the skepticism in his voice haunted me for years.

I wasn't done with education. Something had to be done for the kids in my classes who read and wrote far below grade level. That led me to author Jack Trelease and his Read Aloud Handbook. I would read copiously to my children.

I became a regular at Chester Park Elementary PTA meetings and was invited to become secretary only to have the offer conveniently forgotten. I always suspected rumors of my teaching failures gave someone second thoughts.

That didn't stop me. I was a room parent, read to classes, led Junior Great Books groups and became the games chairman of the newly organized school carnival. My enthusiasm would lead to my first-grade son forbidding me from ever visiting his class again. I had worn a Ninja Turtle mask in every classroom to invite everyone to the new carnival. My son was mortified, a condition he endured until graduation 12 years later.

My greatest success was the maze I constructed out of 30 cardboard appliance boxes. It returned annually until Chester Park closed.

Just two years after losing my last job I would run for the school board and I had a cause. A referendum for new schools and repairs was offered to Duluth voters. I wrote an impassioned op-ed in favor of it in the Tribune. But when it was defeated the school board decided to close Washington Junior High, where I had taught in 1984.

I was appalled. I circulated a petition that garnered several thousand signatures to offer an excess levy to fund the school's continuance. When my toothless petition was ignored by the board I was infected with the common malady – distrust of the powers-that-be.

My 1989 run for the board didn't make it out of the primary. It would be followed by two more defeats. In these campaigns I mailed painfully earnest evaluations of public education to several hundred of Duluth's most influential leaders. I hoped to generate buzz. I got a yawn.

I ran for Congress as an Independent candidate in 1992. I had no record to run on, no money, no party but I'd set my eye on Congress as a college intern working for Minnesota's Republican Congressman Ancher Nelson. That was 1971, the same year that Minnesota's Republican legislators had voted to expand financing for public schools in the "Minnesota Miracle."

By the time I filed for the school board again in 1994 I had six defeats at electoral office under my belt – three for the school board, two for the legislature, and one for Congress. Despite this, I was rescued out of the blue by a couple seasoned pros. Republican Bill Ulland and his Democratic buddy Patty McNulty offered to be my campaign managers. There was one condition. I was to do exactly what they said. They didn't want a repeat of my juggling tennis balls on the debate stage. I gladly agreed. They put their names on the line, raised money, and got me elected. I did break my promise to them in one detail.

While a candidate myself, I became the unofficial manager of another school board candidate's campaign. Before filing I'd heard rumors that an African American woman, Mary Cameron, might run for the 2nd district seat I had my heart set on. Duluth hadn't had a black elected official for almost 20 years. I called Mary up to have a cup of coffee. If she wanted it I planned to offer her the smaller district seat and run, once again, for the city-wide at-large seat that I had already lost three times. To my relief Mary planned to run at-large.

We were both elected and became thick as thieves until the Red Plan. We had a lot in common. For a start, Mary graduated from Duluth's Central High in 1969 the same year I graduated from Mankato High. Central's Basketball team had defeated Mankato for third place in the 1968 Minnesota Basketball Tourney.

On election night my daughter, now in seventh grade, was asked what it felt like to have her dad win an election (his seventh): My daughter put it succinctly. "Well," she explained, "I won't have to wear a paper bag over my head in school tomorrow."

Harry Welty digs up old fossils at: lincolndemocrat.com.

Sculpting Bill Clinton
Snowbizz.com

Snow Bill

In 1992 at the height of my Republican apostasy I threw my support to Bill Clinton. In the process I managed to alienate myself from Republicans and the Reform Party members who stayed loyal to Ross Perot despite the increasing evidence of his quirky paranoia. Since local Democrats had never had any use for me I was pretty effectively in political limbo. Big deal. That meant I was squarely in the middle with about 75% of the population that was fed up with "politics as usual."

After he was inaugurated in 1993 I decided to offer the new President an olive branch. I began to build a snow sculpture bust of the new President. I had never sculpted a face before but I was growing more and more confident of my snow carving abilities.

By coincidence, I got a call from Paul Guggenheimer a reporter for the local CBS affiliate. He told me he wanted to do a story about me for a new series that they were going to call "On the Road." The fluffy piece written about me the previous year by Jeff Potts in Twin Ports People may have drawn Paul's attention to me. It would be a local version of Charles Kurralt's national program by the same name. It would be a two part interview rolled into one. He would show the before and after.

I piled all the snow in my yard into an eight foot high stack on our front lawn overlooking the busy thoroughfare below. Paul and his cameraman shot me piling up the snow up and throwing water on it to make it sticky. You could hear me whistling on the tape. He showed me consulting a dozen photos of Clinton clipped from various magazines. I started adding a protuberance for Bill's nose but I wanted to wait until the weather warmed up and the snow would be snowball sticky. Then I could work it like clay rather than marble. Fortunately, before Paul came back a nice heat wave hit Duluth.

When I finished Bill's face actually had a passable resemblance to the new President. Guggenheimer returned and did a follow-up interview. His story made me look like an affable eccentric and ran nationwide on local stations. I heard from a half a dozen people across the country who had seen it.

The funniest message I got was from a couple of college guys in Ohio who wanted some pointers on snow sculpting because a major snow storm was bearing down on the state.

Bill's head sat patiently on my lawn until I heard about a snow sculpting contest sponsored by local radios station WEBC. I decided to give my Bill a saxophone and enter the contest. I took fourth place! I never saw my competition but I chalked the poor showing up to the fact that WEBC aired Rush Limbaugh's talk show. I don't think they wanted to risk offending their listening audience by giving out an award to a Bill Clinton sculpture.

Then Chuck Curtis, the Duluth Tribune's photographer, added to my celebrity. He took a picture of a passerby gazing up at my statue. It made the AP wire. At least a dozen letters with clippings from papers all over the country of my sculpture were mailed to me.

Not everyone liked my Bill, of course. Someone sneaked up in the middle of the night and knocked off his nose. I got it repaired just in time for a photographer from the Minneapolis Trib who drove up to take pictures of it. They had a nice spread of Bill in their paper the following weekend.

Bill Comes to Duluth

Five years later, on November 4th, 1998, Bill Clinton made a visit to Duluth. He was trying to stem the conservative tide which was about to sweep the Congress. The arrival of a President in town is always a big deal. The visit of JFK to Duluth back in the early 60's, for instance, is a regular subject of pictorial reviews in the local paper. Now a new President was about to pay us a call.

I didn't pay much attention to the Clinton visit, although I kept hearing enthusiastic reports about it from the College Republicans. They were planning to run some kind of relay around the Holiday Inn where the President was to advertise their displeasure with him. It was both silly and fun.

On the day after his arrival in Duluth, and the day he was to speak at the University of Minnesota - Duluth, I was busy working at my computer. When I glanced out the window I noticed a dark, suspicious, figure standing along the avenue standing and facing the avenue. My curiosity piqued I went outside for a closer look. There were more such figures lining the street all they way down the hill to Superior Street four blocks away. Then it dawned on me, my house was on the the most direct route to the campus from the Presidential Suite downtown. The President's motorcade would be passing right by my house.

I noted the time and made a quick calculation. I called Woodland Junior High School and asked for the principal, Ed Marsman. As a newly elected school board member I had no doubt that Ed would honor my request. I told Ed about the sentries, and the presidential route, then asked if it would be all right for me to take my kids out of school for an half hour to watch the President drive by. Ed graciously acceded to my request.

When I arrived at the school a few minutes later my daughter and son were waiting for me in the Principal's office. They were wondering what the heck I had called them out of class for. When I told them they both objected. The Principal, himself, had called them out of class. Now everybody thought they were in trouble. They were mortified.

My daughter, Keely, was more forgiving. My son Robb, was really peeved. He had forbidden me from ever coming to his class again in first grade. That year I had been a co-chairman of the school carnival.

Robb was adamant. He would not watch the President. It was all I could do to order him home. He told me he would stay in the house as the President drove by. I believed him. When he was six he had locked himself in the bathroom for forty five minutes just before we were scheduled to fly out of Duluth on a trip to Disney World. I had only gotten him to open the door by threatening to take the door off its hinges. (That would have been a neat trick because the hinges were on his side of the door. He was only six and his grasp of mechanics had yet to develop) He's a stubborn kid! Rather than argue with him I told him that it was his decision whether to hide from the motorcade or not but that he still had to come home with me.

Republicans had been vilifying the President ever since his inaugural but I was raised to respect the office of Commander and Chief. To be honest, I still had a fair amount of respect for his ideas. As far as I was concerned he was my kind of Republican. Welfare reform, free trade, paying down the national debt, making abortions legal, safe, and rare; these ideas all appealed to me. Of course, that is not how my party viewed him. They blamed him for stealing their best ideas. But my philosophy is simple: When you see a good idea you should steal it - except where copyright law is concerned.

We got to the house and, sure enough, my son headed for his room. Keely stood outside and waited patiently. I went in and grabbed my camera.

I couldn't help wondering if the President would notice my house. It was possible that if someone from the area was driving with him they would mention my snow sculpture of him. It also seemed likely that because my sculpture's photo had been in so many newspapers someone would have shown it to him. In fact, on the day of his arrival in Duluth our local newspaper had made up a humorous list of the top 10 sites that the President ought to visit while in the City. My house was number 8 on the list with a warning to the President about my political affiliation.

When I saw the first flashing light at the bottom of the avenue where the highway fed into it, I rushed to the house and yelled: "The first police car just turned up the hill. The President will be here in less than thirty seconds." Then I returned to the sidewalk. Shortly before the presidential limousine drove past I looked over my shoulder and saw my son's head poking out of the spirea bush overlooking the procession. I quickly looked into my camera and snapped a picture of the limousine as it passed. I never did see the President and my photograph ended up being too blurry to see him in it either.

But my son....."I saw the President!" he said with great animation, "He smiled at me," Ah, those were beautiful words to hear from my son the cynic.

Impeach Clinton

Four years later President Clinton was under fire for his dalliance with an intern, lying to a grand jury, and for being insincerely genuine to the American public. The Republicans were rabid and the public, me included, recoiled as we watched them root around in the President's privy.

My son, now an eighth grader, had just learned how to take an image from our computer and transfer it to an iron-on patch. He toiled for a day on a personal project. When he was done he proudly showed us his creation. He had placed an "Impeach Clinton" sticker on a shirt. We wouldn't let him wear it to school. Refusing to let my son exercise his First Amendment rights made me feel very awkward. I felt like I was giving Bill Clinton aid and comfort that he little deserved at my son's expense.

I'd prefer to have an idealistic son, one like Bill Clinton must have been when he shook hands with John Kennedy. I'd hate to think that Bill Clinton's legacy for my son is an entrenched and inalienable cynicism.

America deserved something better from the President.

Like Father Like Son
Not Eudora   By Harry Welty
Published Aug. 8, 2003

When my son was in First Grade I became the Chairman of the Games Committee for Chester Park's School Carnival. Having fond memories of my own elementary school carnivals I was well suited to the job. It was Chester's first ever carnival and we wanted to make sure all the children would badger their parents to attend. To that end I dressed up as a teenage mutant ninja turtle and went to every classroom, including my son's, to promote the carnival. That night my son told me, in no uncertain terms, that I was never to visit any classroom of his again.

The children of public officials, like those of ministers, often have crosses to bear. Expected to exemplify the noble truths their parents espouse they find themselves tugging at a shorter leash than other children. Few things are more entertaining to watch than children who fail to live up to their parent's lofty ideals. This certainly holds true for the children of school board members.

Every teacher's contract negotiated, every decision about buildings to be closed or referendums to be offered or school bus routes to be rerouted becomes an opportunity to share opinions with the School Board member's child. When it became common knowledge, for instance, that I was about to destroy the district's music program my happy and well adjusted daughter kicked a balustrade out of our banister. One of her fellow students had commented during the history class that it was a shame that the School Board didn't care about kids.

In the brief time that I have followed Duluth school politics two board members have switched their children to private schools and another to a charter school. One Board member's child had a teacher pass out a petition for her father's recall while another's was told by his teacher that she hated his father.

Though both of my children have now mercifully graduated from the Duluth Schools my son had to live his entire school life in the shadow of a mutant ninja turtle school board father. There was my feud with the teacher union's President (since patched up) and my resignation as School Board Chair. There was some voodoo and a little public cursing. As they say, "what goes around comes around."

On the last day of my son's "middle school" career I got a call from the Assistant Principal. My son had been suspended for the last three hours of the school year for starting the mother-of-all food fights. Long planned by the students as a celebration it almost didn't come to pass because the staff had been forewarned. Teachers ringed the cafeteria so that no prudent child was willing to cross the cafeteria floor to turn off the lights. This move had been the preplanned signal to start the festivities while providing students the anonymity of darkness. One student was not, however, too encumbered with his fellow student's prudence.

I still hear about that food fight, five years past. It must have been a doozie. I was recently gratified to hear my son comment sympathetically about the rotten conditions under which lunch room helpers work. They are part time, underpaid and without authority or respect yet they have the responsibility to monitor careless students since most teachers have long since sloughed off this onerous duty. This was exactly the point I tried to impress on my son after the dust, or rather the vegetables, had settled. It was the poor food service personnel who had to pick up afterwards.

Unfortunately, my son's eighth grade year wasn't quite over. He informed me that he still had to turn in a science report or he wouldn't go on to high school. Since he couldn't return to the school I would have to turn it in for him. Under the circumstances going to Woodland Junior High was about the last thing I wanted to do.

I walked into the building praying not to be seen by any of the staff. To my relief the building seemed empty. I walked down the hall to the science class only to find it empty as well. The teacher was gone. As I turned back and passed by the now clean cafeteria I saw the Assistant Principal standing by the lunch counter. Most of the Woodland faculty was sitting in the corner of the cafeteria having lunch.

Putting on my best game face I walked over to the Assistant Principal to ask him if he could help me get my son's papers to the science teacher. He took the papers and told me he'd be happy to give them to her. Suddenly the cafeteria went black just as it had the previous day when my son turned off the lights.

After a lot of tittering in the dark from the teacher's corner the lights were turned back on. Having completed my mission I walked over to the teachers and shrugged. "What can I say," I told them. "Like father like son."

Welty is a small time politician who lets it all hang out at www.snowbizz.com

Resolution

Thursday Dec. 29th, 2022

Harry sculpted his latest reason for remaining resolute in the face of global threats - his angelic granddaughter Charlotte.

"Resolution" is a word that has been made lifeless by its casual use at New Years. It calls to mind quickly abandoned diets or self improvement regimes.

Lost is the sense of determination or the resolution to solve thorny problems. We have those in spades today. If we can't lose weight how can we save the Earth?

Today eight billion of us face a sixth extinction driven by our need to pave over and Formula 409 the planet, making it uninhabitable for rest of God's Ark.

Earth nearly came to a bad end when I was a kid and there were three billions of us facing a reckoning with $E=MC^2$.

Back then, Americans had a literate President who was reading Barbara Tuchman's Guns of August. It was a book about the blind leaders who stumbled into a world war none of them had ever wanted. We are ripe for resolution once again.

I don't make resolutions on New Years but I do make them when sufficiently motivated. Learning French is a recent one. Writing books is another.

Yet to be achieved is a star-spangled resolution to accomplish something useful as a politician.

"Accomplishment" is the the key word. I have no use for the maxim most politicians live by, "The first job of a politician is to get elected."

Hell, Trump got elected and he damned near broke America.

At present I'm mostly a perennial candidate and bloviator. It's not much to write home about but slowly and surely through life resolve, if not success, has taken hold of me.

My parents put my war hero grandfather on a pedestal for me. Risking death was part of his charm.

There were less fearsome encouragements too. In 1960 Democrat, Jack Kennedy, was running against Republican Richard Nixon for president.

Jack's famous hanger-on, Frank Sinatra, had a hit song which became the candidate's unofficial campaign song. It was

"High Hopes."

Each verse describes an impossible task like "a little old ant" moving a rubber tree plant or a ram wanting to "punch a hole in a billion kilowatt dam."

They may have seemed impossible, like electing the nation's first Catholic president, but like Jack Kennedy the song's critters succeeded.

While optimism might fuel resolution it won't necessarily sustain or reward it. As Einstein may have said "Insanity is doing the same thing over and over and expecting different results."

My dad once blew his military severance, to my mother's horror, to start publishing a magazine called "The Optimist." He got three subscribers and published exactly one issue. Lesson learned but perhaps too well (says the son who has run for political office 20 times). Dad found other fish to fry.

Our lives are our testament and the resolution behind some lives have been spectacular.

Martin Luther King Jr and Lyndon Johnson teamed up and finally got black citizens the vote they had a theoretical right to.

When the assassinated Kennedy's advisers told LBJ that trying to pass the legislation was a waste of effort Lyndon's reaction was sterling. If I can't do that, what's the point of being President, he snorted.

Resolution got that job done but it was only a beginning. After 300 years black Americans are still subjected to Klansmen and "Karens" who raise hell when their children sell lemonade on street corners.

My 20 runs for elective office are humorous, even to me, but they are also as deadly serious as public education, honoring the proclamation of equality written into our founding documents and saving the Earth.

I hope I'm not Einstein's idiot but if I am I don't plan to

quit.

I write a weekly column for a tabloid to an unknown audience which is as silent to me as I am to the hundreds of people whose work I read every day.

Licking my wounds from last year's congressional loss is the last thing I'm interested in. I am still paying attention to the fellow I challenged three times.

I read that Mr. Stauber didn't make an appearance when the brave leader of the Ukraine gave an address to Congress before Christmas. It was Pogo who said, "We have met the enemy and he is us."

And while I'm quoting other luminaries here's some vintage Teddy Roosevelt: "It is not the critic who counts: not the man who points out how the strong man stumbles or where the doer of deeds could have done better. The credit belongs to the man who is actually in the arena, whose face is marred by dust and sweat and blood, who strives valiantly, who errs and comes up short again and again, because there is no effort without error or shortcoming, but who knows the great enthusiasms, the great devotions, who spends himself in a worthy cause; who, at the best, knows, in the end, the triumph of high achievement, and who, at the worst, if he fails, at least he fails while daring greatly, so that his place shall never be with those cold and timid souls who knew neither victory nor defeat."

I second that motion.

Welty also shoots his mouth off at lincolndemocrat.com.

Seeing through my daughter's eyes
Published July 6, 2005

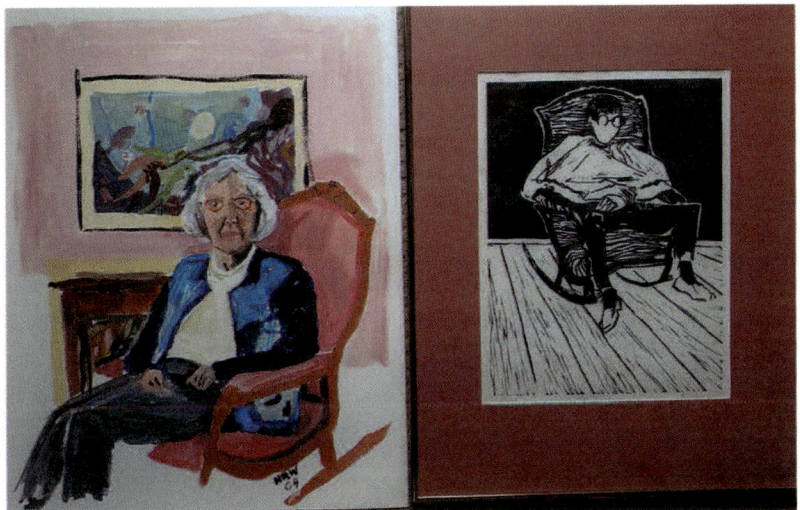

George Robb's Lincoln rocker in a pen and ink drawn by his daughter, Georganne, of her son, Harry, and the rocker painted 38 years later by Harry in acrylic of his mother.

After my daughter Keely was born in the spring I took my visiting mother-in-law Shirley out to a sandwich shop for lunch. It was the only time in the eight years I knew her that we got to talk, just the two of us. Shirley was a sharp spirited and saucy woman. That fall Shirley was killed when her small plane crashed while flying to Duluth to witness Keely's baptism. It was a time of many tears.

As a consequence of the tragedy Keely's baptism was delayed for some years but she was a regular at "children's time" during church services. On one such occasion our pastor asked the children to tell him what foods were eaten by the Pilgrims and Wampanoag Indians at the first Thanksgiving. The children volunteered the predictable fare; turkey, corn, potatoes and then Keely loudly and confidently suggested "bacon." The Church burst out in a congregational guffaw at this unexpected reply. Keely stood and looked out at the congregation with injury in her eyes. "They laughed at me!" she cried out reducing the congregation from mirth to shame as she fled from the pastor. With a mixture of sympathy and embarrassment we scooped her up and took her to the hallway so that she wouldn't disrupt the service. "When I grow up," she sobbed, "I'm going to wreck this church!" Keely was and remains spirited much like her lost grandmother. She has yet to make good on her threat.

When Keely was about ten we settled down to watch the musical "West Side Story." Keely was sitting on my lap as the opera's young hero was felled in a street fight. Keely began trembling, her body wracked by sobs. I too began to cry in empathy. The darned thing about crying is that its convulsions are almost indistinguishable from those of laughter. Sensing that I was responding to her dismay with mirth Keely fled from my lap. Just as with the Thanksgiving bacon Keely did not want anyone to find amusement in her dismay.

Keely grew up with a single grandmother, my mother, Georganne. As Shirley was spirited my Mother was gracious and this too has been one of my daughter's attributes.

For several years my mother has been overtaken by Alzheimer's disease and recently her children had to find other accommodations for her. Last week when I told Keely that I would be visiting town to help repaint my mother's old apartment she announced that she had two days off and that she would come over to help me.

Keely is two-years married now and no longer a part of our daily lives so it was a special treat for me to spend two days working side by side with her. She is a hard worker and better yet a cheerful one. Keely's grandmother was an artist and we took great care in removing mom's paintings from the walls as we prepared to paint them. Prepping the wall was rather like the preparations my mother made for the many art projects she set up for her grandchildren.

After our first day's work I planned to look in on my mother at her new residence. I have visited mom regularly for the past several months and witnessed her precipitous decline. I expected to find that the new and unfamiliar environment of a residential treatment center had intensified her confusion. I knew I would have to carry the "conversation" as even before our visit my mother had been reduced to asking her guests repeatedly, "What city is this?" and "Where are we?"

Keely sat on a rumpled bed, in the Spartan room, that is the final residence of the only grandmother she has ever known. I sat opposite them on mom's "Lincoln rocker" which was brought to the room to lend it some semblance of familiarity. I told mom how much I liked the chair. She narrowed her eyes and told me it wasn't the Lincoln Rocker. I remained upbeat and didn't disagree. I prattled on mentioning the names of relatives trying to rekindle mom's memories while keeping awkward silence at bay. For minutes I blathered as though oblivious to my own mother's vacuity.

Soon I noticed that my normally ebullient daughter was silent. I glanced over and saw her bravely trying to join the conversation as tears welled up in her eyes. She could not speak. Her grandmother, my mother, had altogether disappeared such was the brutality of her illness. The frail, confused soul who had given us both life and unqualified love no longer knew us. My steady voice began to catch as tears welled up in my eyes too. I looked at the floor to prevent them from spilling down my cheek. I saw that mom's shoes were on the wrong feet and gratefully knelt down to switch them around and so hide my unwelcome emotion. My voice cracked as I tried to tease mom about her shoes. Seeing her Father cry only made Keely's tears fall more freely. We were a mess.

When I was a young man I trained myself, as was the fashion, to be stoic. I would not let sentiment dampen my eyes. Through the years my daughter has helped save me from this false bravado by teaching me that it is as pointless as a palette of black and white.

Welty is a small time politician who lets it all hang out at: www.snowbizz.com

Sending a Star to Mom

Posted on December 6, 2014 www.lincolndemocrat.com

Moon Madness, watercolor by Georganne Welty, 1998

And life goes on.

The attendant who came in as I finished singing Good King Wenceslas looked alarmed as she bent toward my mother.

"Has she passed?" I asked her.

"I was just here a few minutes ago" she replied as she tried to feel a pulse. She got a stethoscope and summoned a nurse but that was not going to change anything.

One of the attendants who I'd kibitzed with for the four years mom had been on the wing entered mom's room in tears. She told me how my mother was her favorite. That's astonishing enough since about all my mother could do was sing a tuneless "Wai, Wai, Wai." This was her duet with me in every song I sang to her. Rarely she might surprise me by saying "I love you." There was no point trying to keep my tears back.

As I left my mother's mortal remains behind in her room I made a couple phone calls. The first was to my estranged sister who had planned to come up the next day to make sure someone was with mom while her heart still beat. She had agreed to travel to Duluth the next day, Saturday, while I traveled with my son-in-law's family for their traditional Winter get-together. My daughter, Josh's new wife and the mother of his two new boys, couldn't make the trip because she's taking a once-a-semester two-day class in the Twin Cities for her otherwise online class. Neither could Claudia because she had a Friday Class at her Seminary which was also in the Twin Cities. They would be gone for two nights leaving my new son-in-law with two rambunctious boys. Their overnight absence would cost them both to miss seeing little Jacob's preschool production of the Disney movie "Frozen." They would have to catch it on video which new dad, Josh, would record before departing solo for his Company Christmas party. The planning for this busy day had left the boys in my care for the night. Moreover, I had been asked at the last minute to be a replacement "narrator" by the Preschool of the Fine Arts.

In fact, I had only popped in to see my gravely ill mother that morning for a quick check to see how she was doing. I was scheduled to head over to the school for one final full dress rehearsal before that evening's performance. I had just experienced the curtain closing on one show while the next was was preparing for a final early morning dress rehearsal.

At my mother's passing my sister's desire to visit ceased with mom's final heartbeat. I told Becky of my near miss having arrived for a lone Christmas carol during which mom passed. Becky told me of a premonition. The previous night she and her ex, a long-time caretaker of my mother, her son, my namesake, all simultaneously began playing solitaire.

She recalled that my mother had played the game ad infinitum while they all lived together. She told me that she felt mother's spirit in the room as they all played cards. Such were the thoughts of our family's Buddhist and they weren't much different than mine, as an agnostic.

I called my brother Andy next and relayed to him my sister's thoughts on next steps that would be required. This was a longer call. By now I was in my car prepared for a race to the morning rehearsal but I found myself "bridged." I was stuck in traffic. It's a phenomenon unique to Duluth, Minnesota's Park Point the Earth's longest fresh water sand bar. The peninsula was severed from Duluth by a canal a hundred years ago. For decades it has remained connected to the mainland by its Ariel Lift Bridge that raises its span to admit ships into St. Louis Bay behind the sandbar. A half mile of cars was stopped while a big Canadian Ore boat cruised into our harbor. That was when the funeral parlor answered my call. I explained that I would be back to see my mother near noon because of my pressing need to rehearse for my grandson's holiday program. I would meet their staff a few hours later when they could pick mom up. Although mom had died at 9:30 AM the funeral home would record her passing as having taken place at 10:15 when an actual nurse was available to confirm the fact.

As the Bridge lowered its span about to release me from the Point I had one more call to make. It was to my wife Claudia, and my daughter, Keely. They were en route to the Twin Cities. When I reached Claudia she asked how things were. She understood from the previous evening that the end was near. Upon learning that mom had died she began sniffling. Claudia asked how I was doing. "Fine," I stammered, "Until I talked to you." It was just the second instance of many more tears that I would shed throughout the day.

I had gotten up early that morning to make alterations to the pre-school script adding in stage directions that coincided with my narration. My initial phone calls complete I parked beside Trinity Lutheran Church the site of the preschool. My grandson, perhaps the most easily distracted child in the program, was very keen to see me. He showered me with glances and waves as he stood steadfast in the square his teachers had taped to the floor to keep him confined. Other children only required a short strip of tape with their names on them to remain tethered.

By noon I was free to drive to the funeral parlor to transact business. As my brother and I are co-conservators I had to call him again to fax his signature for the paperwork. It had been agreed by all of us that mom would be cremated and that there would be no funeral as the few people who knew her lived in Mankato a town she had not lived in for nearly a quarter century. Eventually we would lay her ashes to rest beside our Father.

It was well past two when I pulled into the nursing home just ahead of the funeral parlor's staff. Some conversations with Bayshore Care employees were necessary and I wanted to load mom's art and family photos and get them home leaving me enough time to change into a suit and tie. Last minute jitters had the teachers thinking they might need a fourth rehearsal before the scheduled performance.

I began loading our car as the undertakers arrived. Before my second load they were placing mom on a gurney for the trip to their vehicle. I had been at my dad's side too when he had been wheeled off in the same manner 27 years earlier. My mother had not been whole for almost a decade but now, like my father, she was fully absent.

I emptied the room with a couple more loads and had fifteen minutes to race home and grab a coat and tie. I'd have to unload the car after the big show and cram two small boys in with all the keepsakes. The boys would be in my charge while their dad was at his company dinner. The next day I would have to get them ready for our Saturday trip to have yet another Holiday party with their dad's family in Central Minnesota.

A fateful thought crossed my mind as I pulled up to the church. The boys and I could make our evening a night to remember my mother. I decided we would watch the Wizard of Oz on our unopened DVD celebrating its 70th Anniversary.

Claudia was convinced that Margaret Hamilton would be too intense for Jacob and had repeatedly scolded me every time I suggested the boys watch it with us. She was sure Jacob would get nightmares. Aw Heck. The previous spring I had both boys paint the Wicked Witch green when I sculpted her in snow. Now Claudia was safely out of town and couldn't stop me.

My mother was a Kansas girl and had checked every Oz book out of the library. As a young mother she had read half a dozen of the books to me. For our movie snack I had the treats I kept my mother's room stocked with for the last four years, Hershey's Kisses. I'd spent a small fortune keeping her Papier-mache' candy bowl perched on an elephant full of them. I thought they would tempt the staff in to check on my mom. Tonight it would be my grandson's turn to sample the many flavors I brought back with me.

I reread my narration to make sure I had all the cues in the right order but otherwise had to cool my heals until the four O'clock start. In the meantime, I found Grandma Sue, the mother of new dad Josh, in the audience. She had staked out one of the seats near the left front where I'd texted her son it would be the best place to shoot a video of the production. My camcorder was new having only been used once before to record one of my wife's Sunday school classes. Claudia was teaching it for one of her Seminary courses. She got a 97 out of 100. Damn shame she's taking all her classes pass/fail.

A few minutes after four there was standing room only and a crisis. Our Olaf, the little snowman, got stage fright. He had to be replaced necessitating a costume change, carrot and all. After ten minutes an apology was offered for the delay. Then the understudy got stage fright and more time passed. I sat by the stage door clueless as to the frantic work behind the scenes. I tried to mollify the crowd by joking about first day jitters. Then, finally, the cast entered en masse with its new snowman. It wasn't the understudy. It was Jake with a magnificent orange carrot sticking out above his forehead. I gave him a big smile and surreptitious thumbs up. The first number was a full cast sing-a-long but a minute in I looked at Jacob and saw a small stricken child held captive by his square. Jacob/Olaf had tears streaming down his face as the other children sang and gyrated. The gravity of his situation had sunk in deep.

Jacob needed an arm around his shoulder but I was helpless. I couldn't wade into the cast. My reassuring and sympathetic look wasn't slowing the tears. I motioned him over to me and he threaded his way through the cast and hugged me while I whispered that he could do it. I shooed him back to his square as the first song concluded and cast evaporated for the first scene. Jake's teachers directed him to a hiding place behind a cardboard mountain he had not hidden behind in any of his three rehearsals. I could only hope he could steel himself to the task of remembering the unpracticed lines that had given the first two snowmen cold feet.

Teacher Jodi had assured me beforehand that this performance would be "preschool perfect" and she was right. At the rehearsal Princess Elsa was dragged to jail by the guards. The audience, however, was treated to five guards picking the princess up by each appendage and carried precariously to her incarceration. I never figured out what the fifth guard was holding on to but the audience was biting its nails.

There was a daring jail break and an escape to the mountains leading to Olaf's grand entrance and first spoken line. My little Olaf emerged from his mountain all smiles. "Yeah, why?" he inquired successfully and smiled even more broadly. He got laughs so, for good measure, he said it a second time. The crowd's mirth was intoxicating and a thespian was born that night.

At the conclusion of the performance loud applause rang through the church basement. The lights were dimmed and candles were passed out for the singing of Silent Night. Although I hadn't brought anything for the potluck dinner that followed I surrendered to my grandsons, especially Jake who wanted to stay with the other kids. There was plenty to eat.

After dinner I grabbed the string dangling from one of the helium balloons that decorated the set and handed it to Jacob. It was a shiny silver star. It caught on my coat and was almost pulled out of his hands before we left the church. I offered to hold it until we got to the car but Jake was determined to be its bearer. We walked out to the bright night lit by a full moon. As I began to explain to my grandsons the special night I had planned to honor my mother who had just departed for heaven I teared up once more. As we neared the car I heard an anguished wail. I turned to see Jacob's silver star ascending into the heavens.

I told the boys the first thing that occurred to me. What we were seeing was very special. Jacob had just sent a star up to meet my mother who had left for heaven a little earlier that day. By the time we were getting buckled into the car older brother Tanner was crying too. First he cried in sympathy for his brother's loss and then at the news of my mother's death. It took me a while to restore calm while I choked back tears. When I regained my composure I told the boys about my plans for the night and explained that we were going to watch "The Wizard of Oz." I told them they had to keep it a secret from grandma because she was worried that the movie would give Jacob nightmares.

By the time we reached our house equanimity had begun to prevail. I took a small plastic Christmas tree out of the car leaving everything else behind. We hurried down to the basement. I put up the little Christmas tree that I'd decorated the previous night for my mother. The boys took a quick bath so that they would be clean and fresh for their dad's family gathering the next day. This required a little more work as our hot water wasn't working. I had to haul a couple buckets of hot water up a couple flights of stairs to warm up the tub. When they were scrubbed and clean I let each boy choose a handful of my mom's Hershey's kisses to snack on in our journey to Oz.

Tanner, who had seen the movie a year earlier, warned little brother Jake when it would get scary and Jake shielded his eyes but not for long. To my delight, he was mesmerized by the story. I sat with a boy on either side of me and a fat yellow cat on my lap. Tanner explained that the Kansas scenes were in black and white. I told the boys how my mother had grown up in Kansas, not far from Dorothy's home, and how she had read the Oz books to me when I was their age.

When the movie ended I read a couple books to the boys and then sang them songs I had once sung to my mother. The boys collapsed an hour later. I did not expect any nightmares.

NOTE TO READERS: I HAVE MEANT TO EDIT THIS POST SINCE FIRST WRITING IT. I FINALLY GOT THE JOB DONE ONE YEAR TO THE DAY THAT MOM DIED. I CONCLUDED THE ORIGINAL POST WITH THESE LAST TWO PARAGRAPHS. "WHEN I'M 64" WILL STILL APPLY TO ME FOR THE NEXT FIVE DAYS.

Sorry, but I'm wrung out again. It's late and there will be no proof reading of this. Although there are more post worthy subjects stuck in my head I'm still planning to abide by my pledge from a few posts ago to shut my fingers down.

One more thing. I've been telling my family I don't want them to sing Happy Birthday when mine rolls around. I want them to sing the Beatles "When I'm 64." I've been waiting for it to be apropos for about fifty years.

From www.lincolndemocrat in the category "Harry's Diary"

I WAS A BROWN KID
1963-1974

("**Brown**" as in *Linda Brown vs. Topeka Board of Education.* My parents moved into a Topeka home where they knew I would soon be part of an integrated elementary school. NOTE:the image above is Ruby Bridges not Linda Brown)

"**Lily white town**" by Georganne Welty circa 1970

      Topeka, Kansas, was a mostly white town. Before we moved to Minnesota we lived next to Tennessee Town, so-called because it had been settled by African Americans fleeing persecution and lynchings from Tennessee in particular.

Mankato, Minnesota was effectively all white or Lily white as my mother painted it. There had been a Jewish haberdasher and a black veterinarian but there would be no black kids an any Mankato classrooms until our family hosted a foreign exchange student from Africa in 1967. That was the year the Supreme Court struck down Virginia's law making inter-racial marriage a crime.

Bedru

Published May 26, 2005

Bedru Beshir Mohammed Desta Beshir 1948-?*
*** Note follows story**

There is a story about Bedru that I would tell if I knew for certain that he was dead. But Eritreans are a proud people and should my telling of the tale ever come to his attention I could not be sure that he would forgive me. He held fast to one grudge back in 1968 the year he lived with my family. A teacher's innocent remark which made a classroom burst out laughing burned in Bedru's heart until the end of the school year. Mr. Wilker, one of my favorite teachers, was crushed at year's end to receive Bedru's angry letter accusing him of racism.

Years later when I tried to learn my old roommate's fate I discovered that my mother had thrown out all the letters he had sent my parents after his return to Ethiopia. They made her feel guilty as though our family had abandoned him. We did. This was the last thing I could have expected when our local AFS Program (American Field Service) announced that no families had volunteered yet to host the next year's male foreign exchange student.

I don't know what possessed me to ask my parents if they would be willing to be hosts. I was dumbfounded when we filled out the application. When my mother expressed reservations about answering "yes" to the question about our willingness to host a student from a different race the rest of us shamed her into going along. Not long afterwards we were informed that our student would be from Ethiopia. He would be an African. Not only that, he was also a Muslim. Never in anyone's memory had Mankato High School enrolled a black student or for that matter a Muslim.

We picked Bedru up in the Twin Cities shortly before school started and peppered him with questions on the drive home that he could not answer. However well he could read English he could barely speak it. It would take a few months before he was fluent enough to get by and it was probably during this time that he concluded Mr. Wilker had mocked him in front of his classmates.

Bedru was smothered with a lot more "Minnesota Nice" than racism in Mankato. I once saw an acquaintance mouth "Black Boy" as he stared at Bedru in a crowded hallway but I was the only one who noticed. Most Mankato kids were simply curious about our exotic guest. We didn't have any snow that year (if you can believe that!) but a gang of sophomores took him snowmobiling on a frozen lake. Poor Bedru only wore leather street shoes on that expedition and got very cold toes. It was another escapade, this time with some of Bedru's fellow seniors, that I can't bring myself to write about. But even here juvenile curiosity seems to have played more of a role than anything mean-spirited.

While racism was not an overwhelming factor in his stay it was a factor. Bedru's attraction to a cheerleader was awkward. She reluctantly agreed to go to a movie with him even though she had a steady boy friend. She didn't want Bedru to think she was a racist. This was the kind of racism we encountered; the kind where people bent over backward to prove they weren't racists. To her credit Pam was probably the first white girl to "date" a black man publicly in Southern Minnesota during an era when a dozen states would have jailed them for breaking the law. However, there were limits. When he asked her if she wanted to kiss him she declined. That would have been disloyal to her boyfriend. Bedru was a little put out after the date probably because he had gotten a lot of his ideas about western women from characters in the James Bond movies he'd seen back in Ethiopia, characters like Pussy Galore.

Although my family had placed an arrow facing Mecca on the floor of our bedroom Bedru told us that the Prophet excused traveling Muslims from praying while in foreign lands. I got the impression that Bedru felt he could store up his neglected prayers and fulfill them all upon his return home. We had one close call over his eating pork during one school lunch but the cooks assured us that the hot dog he'd consumed had been made with beef. Frankly, I don't think he missed his religious duties any more than most kids miss attending Sunday school.

Despite nuisances like frozen toes and mayonnaise Bedru was probably more at ease in Minnesota than he had ever been in Eritrea. He relished our secular freedom. His ambition was simple and universal. He wanted to attend college and make a good life. He hinted strongly that he would have liked to stay in America to attend college. This hope greatly troubled my parents.

Had he been allowed to stay my parents would have felt

obligated to host him for another four years but that's not what they had signed up for. AFS rules spared them this worry. Owing to the reluctance of foreign nations to lose their most talented students in a "brain drain," AFS students were required to return home when their school year ended. My father, a lawyer, held firmly to this part of Bedru's contract. No doubt the INS would have backed him up.

Whatever fate awaited Bedru back home in 1968 it didn't seem a whole lot worse than what was happening in Vietnam War plagued America. In April Martin Luther King Jr. was assassinated and riots broke out in dozens of our largest cities.

Being an African this calamity did not affect Bedru the same way it affected black Americans. Having grown up in Africa with nothing but Africans around him he had not been made to feel inferior to white people. But having been raised in an authoritarian colony Bedru did identify with our nation's democratic evangelism. President Kennedy's Peace Corps program had sent several dozen American volunteers to Bedru's hometown and he greatly admired the martyred President.

When Kennedy's younger brother, Robert, began his charge for the White House Bedru followed his campaign even more avidly than my politics obsessed family. The rest of us went to bed the moment Kennedy's victory in California was announced. Bedru stayed glued to the television. He turned the lights out and went to bed quietly that evening without waking us with the news that he had just seen Bobby Kennedy's murder. He returned to Africa a few days later.

Notwithstanding these horrors Bedru's visit to America gave him a glimpse into a world of possibilities. Sadly, his Minnesota adventure caused him to forfeit his opportunities back in Ethiopia.

Mussolini's conquest of Ethiopia in 1936 was launched from Eritrea an Italian colony on the Red Sea. After the Second World War the UN awarded the "protectorate" of Eritrea to Ethiopia thus giving landlocked Ethiopia a seacoast and a large Islamic minority. Ethiopia was an ancient Christian kingdom.

From the moment of their annexation Eritreans set out to gain their independence.

While in America Bedru was safe from the conflict. He had studied five languages and fully intended to attend the University in Addis Ababa. But while Bedru learned spoken English in the United States his facility with Ethiopia's national language, Amharic, withered. When he took the entrance examinations back home he failed Amharic. His letters to us complained bitterly that less deserving students could gain admittance by bribing government officials.

The day Bedru arrived in Minnesota I had asked him eagerly about his wonderful emperor, Haile Selassie, so famous in the West for his brave but futile stand against Mussolini's invasion. Before the year was over I came to realize that our "hero" was Bedru's oppressor. After taking command of English he remained circumspect about Selassie. There was no telling what kind of dossier Ethiopian agents might be keeping on Bedru, one of their own "foreign" foreign students.

Long after our last letter from Bedru I found a slip of paper with some notes Bedru had jotted down. Some of the notes were written in Triginian his native tongue but he had written down his options in English. His first option was attending the University which of course had not panned out. His second option was to find a job which he was eventually to do. His third option was to join the EPLF. The EPLF was the Eritrean People's Liberation Front. Next to this option Bedru had written the names of five Eritrean friends.

Although the letters to my parents are lost I still have four letters that Bedru sent to me. I'm embarrassed to admit that I didn't write back to him very often. I was too busy enjoying all the opportunities that he was denied. The last letter he sent my parents was mailed in 1972 and it was the one I was specifically looking for. It was oddly vague and read as though he was trying to get it past censors. Since his written English was already labored this letter was very cryptic indeed. He told us that he was in a dark place by himself with only a small friend to keep him company. My mother said it sounded as though he was in jail feeding left over crumbs to a mouse.

The war between the Emperor and the EPLF continued to heat up after Bedru's return. Since educated and ambitious natives are always viewed suspiciously by their colonial masters it wouldn't be surprising if Selassie's government did jail Bedru. The notes I found certainly hinted at his disloyalty. A decade later Selassie himself would be murdered in a coup. A clique of military officers with the ominous sounding acronym, the DIRG, would plunge Ethiopia into an even more rapacious war against Eritrean rebels. They unleashed a man made famine in the mid 1980's which starved a million innocent people to death many of them Eritreans. How Bedru could have survived that decade I can't imagine.

It's been over three decades since Bedru and I shared a room. I've had the luxury to live a life he might have imagined but never got the chance to enjoy. I've tried not to take my good fortune for granted.

Welty is a small time politician who lets it all hang out at: www.snowbizz.com

NOTE: 20 years after I put this remembrance on the Internet on my Snowbizz.com site I got an email from Bedru's nephew in Eritrea. He did not speak English but he had found my recollection and asked a friend to translate it for him. Then he went looking for the author and found me. He confirmed that Bedru had been a "martyr." My family did not know that we were sending our guest to his death in one of the world's too many bleeding nations. Bedru had desperately wanted to stay here and go to college. We had our eyes on a different war.

Lilly
Posted on the blog lincolndemocrat.com August 19, 2011

Topeka, Kansas, was not the South but it was close enough to have a sizeable black population. I was a child there in the Era depicted by the current movie "The Help." I've not seen it but my wife, Claudia, just finished reading the book on which it is based and says it's set in a concentration camp (my exaggeration) but its feel-good enough to paper over the grim reality that was the Civil Rights Era.

I've thought about writing about my own small connection with Lilly, our family's "help" from my youth and this brief reminiscence from Connecticut , another Northern state, has prompted me to add my two cents. I doubt that I'll read The Help but I can think of another book with a movie that does honor to the reality, Harper Lee's To Kill a Mockingbird. It too is a bit of a fantasy. There weren't many Atticus Finches South or North.

Lilly was my mother's age. She lived near the rail road tracks and her children attended the junior high school where my dad's mother (we called her "Nana") taught English. This was Topeka some years after the Supreme Court's Brown decision. Nana was a good person and encouraged a number of her black students, including Lilly's daughter, who she offered a little part-time work helping at her home. After Nana learned that my mother's father was having trouble taking care of himself following the death of his wife, Nana recommended Lilly, her student's mother.

Lilly was single, perhaps divorced or abandoned, and had a gaggle of children. Like the black women of the deep South she could make a little money with menial labor as domestic help. The work was more limited with my grandfather. He was elderly and becoming frail with no children to raise so she didn't become a second mother to his children. His house needed cleaning and he needed someone to cook for him. Like the women working in deep South households Lilly was away from her children when she did my grandfather's chores. She probably did most of her work during the day when her children were in school but there were occasions when my Mother asked Lilly to babysit my brother, sister and me in the evening. She probably relied on her older children to take care of the younger ones in her absence when taking care of us.

Fifty years later I have a sense of the woman she was. She was heavy set, gregarious and a tease. We often played Chinese checkers and I managed to beat her once. I recall reminding her of this and her good natured denial that I had ever beaten her. I was so chagrined.

My grandfather, George Robb, had been a Kansas luminary before his retirement. He served as the State's elected Auditor for 24 years, having been appointed to the office by the Republican Governor. It was a safe appointment because my grandfather was a war hero. He had been awarded one of two Congressional Medals of Honor given to Kansans for service during the First World War. He was not just a war hero either. He earned a master's degree from New York's Columbia University a mighty accomplishment for a boy whose first family home was dug into a Kansas hillside. I'm sure Lilly considered working for such a man as a point of pride.

There was another thing about my grandfather that she would have appreciated – his experiences with African Americans. As a child in the countryside around Salina, Kansas, his family's next door neighbor was an escaped slave who arrived in Salina in the last year of the Civil War. The Robb's were "small d" democrats in their liberal regard for people of all races. They were also loyal Republicans and Abe Lincoln, the man who defeated the South, was their hero. I still have my great grandfather Thomas Robb's copy of the Autobiography of Ulysses S. Grant, Lincoln's hammer.

In 1917 as a thirty-year-old school principal my grandfather volunteered to join the American Expeditionary Force when war was declared on the Kaiser's Germany. He was trained as an officer and sent to France where he awaited a command in the field. When it came it was a big surprise. He was assigned to the French Fourth Army, specifically the 369th Infantry, raised entirely from volunteers from New York, City's Harlem! It was an all Black unit other than its white officers. General Pershing's officer corps, comprised mostly of Southern gentlemen, pressed Pershing to give the New Yorkers to the

French Army which was colorblind after three bloody years of trench warfare.

That same racist American officer corps would not let a single black soldier be awarded the nation's highest military award despite their having served longer in the field than any white American unit. Fortunately, the 369th did have one badly wounded white officer who could be given the medal without embarrassing the South. George S. Robb.

I'm sure my increasingly frail grandfather enjoyed Lilly's respectful sassiness as much as I did. I know they teased each other about baseball. My grandfather listened to Kansas City Athletics games on the radio while Lilly loved Jackie Robinson's Brooklyn Dodgers. That was the first professional baseball team to put a Black star on the roster guaranteeing that it would become black America's favorite team.

I didn't visit my grandfather often when Lilly was present but my mother did and she and Lilly became friends. They talked long and shared their personal lives with each other. My mother told me that Lilly and my grandfather grew very fond of each other. My grandfather was alone and lonely. Lilly had a courtly employer who offered her respect and gratitude.

When my family moved to Minnesota my mother agonized because she felt terribly guilty leaving her father back in Topeka without family to look in on him. For a while Lilly continued on much to my mother's relief but it did not last. Lilly mysteriously disappeared much to my grandfather's dismay. He had no idea why and was at sea without her. It was not long after this that he moved to a senior care facility to live out the rest of his life.

Our family would return to Topeka annually usually in the Summer. On one of our return visits my mother looked up Lilly. It was a painful reunion but my mother learned the reason for Lilly's absenting herself from her father. It was shame.

Lilly had gotten pregnant by a boyfriend. Since she wasn't married she was mortified to have to face my grandfather. That may be hard to believe now but as with Civil Rights it was a different time and place. Lilly had so much respect for my grandfather that she could not face the possibility of his disapproval. She disappeared to preserve her dignity but she ached at her decision.

Lilly told my mother that every year at Halloween she would dress her children up to go trick or treating and drop them off at my grandfather's home to knock on his door while she hid in her car just to see him standing at his doorway.

Lilly and George Robb reached across a great divide enforced by law and stubborn human prejudice to joke and josh and form a deep regard for one another. Topeka, Kansas was hardly the worst place for a black American but its reality was part of the reason why a bright women like Lilly lived by the rail road tracks with little prospect of meeting a man with a job and little prospect for employment other than domestic work.

Topeka, High School did enroll black and white students before Brown vs. Board of Education. It had a black principal and a white principal and separate sports teams. My uncle recalls the black principal's chief responsibility seemed to be to enforce segregation in the otherwise integrated school.

The kinds of employment available for blacks had always been minimal. In 1921 one of Topeka's black residents found himself accused of raping a white girl in Duluth, Minnesota and was hung from a downtown streetlamp the day after he arrived with a traveling circus as a manual laborer. Three men were lynched that day which shocked blacks across the nation as it demonstrated that there was really no safety anywhere in America for them, not even 700 miles north of Kansas.

Today Duluth had a community meeting to come up with ideas to help minority children catch up with their white peers in the Duluth schools. I suspect that if you traced the backgrounds of those students who are black through time you would be hard pressed to find one who wasn't descended from someone in domestic service.

I AM A BROWN ADULT

("Brown" as in *Linda Brown vs. Topeka Board of Education*. My parents moved into a Topeka home where they knew I would soon be part of an integrated elementary school. NOTE:the image above is Ruby Bridges not Linda Brown)

This photo of Central High student Mary Cameron was taken the day after the assassination of Martin Luther King Jr. It ran on the front page of a Duluth News paper. Since an infamous triple lynching in 1922 black citizens kept a wide birth from the City. I was always struck that this very pretty girl never once had a date in high school. It can be lonely being an easily identifiable minority.

Mary Published Jan 8, 2004

Fifty years ago Mary Cameron was kidnapped from her mother and her Mississippi home by her father and brought to Duluth, Minnesota. Back then Mississippi was a hellish world for Black Americans that few today can comprehend. The northern city he escaped to with his daughter was no Eden. It was a city with far fewer Black residents than other northern industrial cities because most of the Black population had fled from it thirty years before in 1920. That was the year that ten thousand white Duluthians lynched three innocent Black men from a downtown lamppost.

Mary and her brothers and sisters grew up in this strangely white town before a more color tolerant society took hold. Soft and vulnerable on the inside, tough on the outside, Mary responded to racial slights with her fists. Last night Mary Cameron was elected Chairman of the Duluth School Board.

As a result of behind-the-scenes maneuvers, Mary's selection was preordained. Laura Condon was not happy about this choice and took the opportunity to nominate a different candidate. Laura's eulogy for her own nominee was really a veiled rebuke of Cameron who, Laura implied, would not work with the Superintendent, or be nice to the public.

It was ironic that Condon would suggest that Mary couldn't work with the Superintendent. Six years ago Mary joined Laura in voting for Almanza, and not with her usual allies, thus guaranteeing Julio's hiring.

However impolitic the rebuke it was not completely without foundation. Mary has a temper. As one of her admirers, however, I would hasten to note that I've never seen Mary's temper flare unless she was addressed with contempt, accusation, or insinuation. Mary is not a good role-model for the kind of "Minnesota Nice" which simply veils hostility.

I introduced myself to Mary after I was told we might be running against each other for the Board. I was so impressed with Mary that I worked on her campaign as well as my own even though she was a Democrat and I was a Republican.

That's when I discovered that Mary was graced with a rare quality for a politician - loyalty. I ran afoul of Duluth's African American men's group because I supported keeping a book with the offensive "n" word in it on the shelves of the Nettleton library. Although she disagreed with me on the merits of the book Mary stood by my side after I was attacked. It cost her votes and strained some of her friendships.

Mary has always voted her own conscience even when it offended her traditional supporters. When she filed for reelection four years ago the President of AFSCME, Alan Netland, dropped by her office. He told her that "everyone" was "disappointed" with her.

Her offense was to have voted to give a charter school a chance to operate in Duluth. Since ISD 709 had a miserable record teaching minority children Mary reckoned that something had to be done. It cost her the DFL endorsement. As if that wasn't bad enough another school board member organized a letter writing campaign which accused her of arrogance and indifference to Duluth. Mary lost the election but she didn't give up. Two years later she ran again and this time she was elected.

Mary has good reason to have a chip on her shoulder. She grew up in a lily-white town with deep prejudices. Many of her classmates felt free to point out that she was different. As recently as last year some Kids drove by and shouted the infamous "n" word at her.

Not all of her siblings survived the ordeal of growing up in Duluth. One of Mary's sisters became a drug addict. An emotionally unstable brother was imprisoned for murder. The verdict on Mary herself wasn't immediately apparent. Striking back got her removed from her home. A few years ago I met Judge Earl Gustafson and his wife, who once let Mary stay at their home. Both of them had fond memories of Mary and remembered her as a girl who held rich promise.

The Mary I know is best reflected by a former neighbor

who fondly recalled how Mary's two boys always shoveled the snow off her sidewalk. I've always felt that this was a better measure of Mary's temperament.

Last night an African-American School Board Chairman and a Hispanic-American Superintendent were at center stage. Both of these people have gone through some pretty rough patches to get where they are. Almanza was enrolled in a tough public school in Chicago before he knew a word of English. He too learned to survive with his fists. Together these two have presided over something of a golden age in the Duluth School District, despite enrollment losses, declining revenue and more controversies than you can shake a stick at. I just hope that the people who address the new school board keep in mind Aretha Franklin's famous refrain: "Show a little R-E-S-P-E-C-T."

Welty is a small time politician who lets it all hang out at: www.snowbizz.com

King for a Day
Published Jan. 2005

Fresh from their victory saving Grant Elementary School the NAACP's Duluth Chapter is lobbying The School Board to honor Martin Luther King. They want school to be closed on his birthday or at least on the Monday closest to his birth. Martin would become, so to speak, King for a Day.

There is an irony in this. During his lifetime Reverend King was a thorn in the side of the NAACP. His alternative organization, the SCLC, (Southern Christian Leadership Conference) and his powerful religious message stole the thunder from the cool, legalistic NAACP. Perhaps this was because King appealed to the heart while the NAACP appealed to reason. Nonetheless, the NAACP had their successes as I discovered at a very tender age.

One day, at the beginning of the 1958 school year, the

teachers of Loman Hill Elementary School in Topeka, Kansas , sent their students out to the playground for an extended recess. Upon my release from the classroom I climbed to the top of the jungle gym.

As I surveyed the world from my perch I spied a long, orderly line of black children heading down the sidewalk toward our school. The youngest children led the way followed by progressively older students. Each child carried his or her own chair and on each chair stood a neat stack of textbooks. It must have been their teachers - their old teachers - who were shepherding them to Loman Hill. The NAACP's triumph, Brown vs. Topeka Board of Education, had the unintended consequence of ending the teaching careers of hundreds of black teachers in Topeka. They were no longer needed to teach black children and the tenure laws gave preference to white teachers.

Although Topeka's school board acceded to the ruling in the Brown case it was an island of sanity. In Little Rock, Arkansas, integration was only accomplished at the point of a bayonet. Throughout the South white families pulled their children out of public school and sent them to newly organized all-white private schools. Private schools were immune from the Supreme Court's ruling on "public" schools. As an added bonus property taxes could be kept low if a community didn't bother with the education of its black children. Since black citizens were largely prevented from voting there wasn't much they could do about the decline of the public schools.

Then the white South sat back smugly and enjoyed watching Northern School Districts explode over the court ordered bussing of children to achieve school integration. America's schools are more segregated today, than they were fifty years ago.

This is not to suggest that times have not changed for the better. Condoleeza Rice, about to become our Nation's Secretary of State, was a nine year old in Birmingham, Alabama when one of her classmates was among the four girls killed in the Ku Klux Klan bombing of a black church. The

Klan was mad. Rev. King had been jailed the previous spring for trying to register the city's fearful black voters.

King's Civil Rights career began by trying to win the same freedom on city buses that white passengers had. Then King worked to give blacks the right to vote. Then he began demanding that the American economy be opened to black Americans. Finally he objected to a war that drafted black men to fight while white boys got college deferments.

King was no more the Civil Rights movement than George Washington was the Revolution or Abraham Lincoln was the Civil War. Rather, the Nation's memory came to see these men as the embodiment of a greater spirit of liberty and justice. Today Washington and Lincoln have their Monday perhaps King should have his too. And yet it's worth pondering whether giving students a day off in Duluth to relax is the best way to commemorate Dr. King.

Martin Luther King once wrote a letter from Birmingham 's Jail to white ministers who were critical of his movement. Among other things he told them that "injustice anywhere is a threat to justice everywhere."

Yes, today we have Condoleeza Rice but we also have one million black men – one in every twelve, sitting behind prison walls. Most of them are poorly educated, most are denied the vote and all of them are out of the nation's economy. Meanwhile, white Americans have moved to the exurbs, successful blacks have moved to the suburbs, and black inner city children wait for their father's paroles. Where is Martin Luther King's justice today?

There's nothing wrong in taking a day off to celebrate Martin Luther King's birth. There is no guarantee that such a holiday will remind us what Martin Luther King lived and died for.

Welty is a small time politician who lets it all hang out at: www.snowbizz.com

Across the Tidal Basin
10th in a series of sights and recollections of DC
Thursday Oct. 5th, 2023

New memorials are a constant along our nation's Mall. Near the end of our tour I got to look at the new addition that I most wanted to see as the sun set and DC's lights winked on.

The towering King who clasps his "I have a Dream Speech" in his hand was unveiled in August of 2011. MLK's stern visage struck me from the beginning as bold and appropriate for a man who faced death every day of his life. That it was carved by a Chinese sculptor at a time when there was amity between our nations seemed fitting too.

The Asian eye caught King perfectly. Its placement on the Tidal Basin, took my breath away.

My only spring trip to Washington took place a few years after the birth of our daughter Keely, whose sons were now following in her footsteps to the Capitol. On that March visit we caught one of the capital's most fetching displays. The thousand cherry trees given to the nation by Japan, long before we fought each other in the Second World War, flower simultaneously.

They were in magnificent bloom on my daughter's first visit. I perched her on a cherry branch below the pink effusion for a photo. My timing couldn't have been better. That night a torrential rain knocked them all off.

Those cherry trees survived our war as I hope the King statue will survive our tense new relationship with China.

Our nation's capital has known many periods of such tension. During the Civil War the Basin was little more than a morass of muddy malarial wetlands where Union troops bivouacked near the Lincoln White House. Of course the president's children couldn't help but visit the camps and the dashing men in blue who were tenting there to protect their father and the union.

And in those pestilential camps Lincoln's favorite, Eddy, caught typhoid fever and died in 1862. His stricken father had no time to grieve as he labored to save the nation.

I don't know what the planners of the King Memorial had in mind but I found my answer to that question in the memorial's placement. King is hidden as you enter from the Lincoln Memorial. He is emerging from a monolith of stone. As you approach you can only see a narrow view of the Tidal Basin. As you pass through its corridor Dr. King emerges from his Biblical mountain, arms crossed staring hard across the Basin. In his line of sight is the memorial to our third president who was, more importantly, the author of our Declaration of Independence.

In the second of the two photos above you see my grandsons as they stare at the Jefferson Memorial. King is behind them looking over their shoulders. From this viewpoint the memorial's columns hide a standing Jefferson.

The walls of his memorial have many of his most famous quotations carved into marble. Of these none is more important than the foundation of the Declaration of Independence on the southwest wall. "We hold these truths to be self-evident, that all men are created equal, that they are endowed by their Creator with certain inalienable rights, among these are life liberty, and the pursuit of happiness…"

I have little doubt that the sculptor, Lei Yixin, studied King and the setting and knew full well that our third president and his words would lay within the gaze of his subject. Jefferson's words are the ones Martin Luther King championed till his martyr's death.

Jefferson lived to a ripe old age, along with the words he betrayed for the rest of his life. His words have outlived him.

Lafayette, the Marquis de La Fayette, the heroic French officer who served Washington returned to France sure that America's rise hailed a new dawn for the world. Years later the Marquis would express regret for having fought for America in the name of freedom and liberty. He grieved, "I would never have drawn my sword in the cause of America, if I could have conceived that thereby I was founding a land of slavery."

My Grandfather, George Robb, a war hero himself, led black soldiers fighting in French trenches during the First World War. You may recall the doughboys call to arms, "Lafayette, we are here!" I always knew that my Grandfather was not a fan of Jefferson but can only speculate as to the reason.

I know this. George Robb wrote with pride about his father Thomas who called himself a "black republican." That was in defiance of the Southern slur for abolitionists. The slur was that era's "n - - - - lover."

I suspect my grandfather's judgment of Jefferson was simple. He was a hypocrite!

The King who faces the Tidal Basin wrote a speech which predicts a day when black children and white children can live together. It's little wonder that he looks hard at the place where our nation's hypocrisy began. God knows when that day will come.

Our recent president, who hopes to return to the White House after his 2021 defeat, once made a grudging 90-second trip to the King Memorial after being criticized for ignoring it. Perhaps that's no surprise from a man who fought the Justice Department when they tried to make him rent his apartments to African Americans and who used his wealth to buy full page ads calling for the execution of five black adolescents for a crime they didn't commit.

At least Jefferson used pretty words.

More from Welty can be found at Lincolndemocrat.com

Why is Michelle Obama in my Basement?
Jan 6, 2022

"Why is Michelle Obama in your Basement?"

That's what my grandson asked me after he crawled back out of the dark, dingy space under our sunroom. At the end of the millennium, when my wife and I became empty nesters, I turned this space into my wine cave. Although he didn't remember it, when he was very little, I would occasionally send him and his older brother in to fetch bottles for me.

For 72 years, before we purchased the house, the space was left unfinished. It still is filled with a dusty clay too dry for earth worms or anything else. The "floor" slopes steeply downward from the street side to the alley side four feet lower. Its only entrance is through a square hole left in the wall of our laundry room. Getting in with my flashlight wasn't easy. It required a step ladder. At my first peek all I saw was some debris that seemed to have been tossed in carelessly perhaps by the masons who laid our home's foundation.

My daughter, now mother of my grandson, has a vivid imagination. She always wondered what lay behind the makeshift wooden blockade that sealed the unseen emptiness behind it. For her 13th birthday party she begged us to let her friends crawl in to explore. I wrinkled my nose in disgust at the thought, but the party guests went in armed with flashlights. They came out with red clay dust under their nostrils. Their prize was a flattened cardboard box used for mailing California oranges. Their eyes widened when they read to whom it had been mailed - Mrs. Charles Welty. That was our name!!! In all the years we'd lived in Duluth only one other Welty had ever been listed in the phone directory and Michelle Welty, whoever she was, only lived in town for a couple years. Only the supernatural could explain this amazing coincidence. And now we learned, we were only our house's second Weltys

When my kids graduated from Duluth East I found a use for this dusty dungeon. I began a competition with my brother over wine. He had developed a love for wine after moving next to California's Napa Valley. We both began to explore the sophisticated world of the oenophile. I suggested cutting a doorway from the laundry room into the space under the sun room. My prudent wife said "no," so I improvised. I leveled the top of the slope and covered its clay with a 4 by 8 foot plank of plywood. It gave me a level surface for wine racks. Lots of wine racks.

I had painted a John McCain sign on this plywood for his Presidential run in 2000 and put it in my front yard. In 2003 my friend and former school board colleague, Mary Cameron, wanted a second go at it. She had lost her re-election bid two years earlier and I was her gung-ho campaign manager. We ordered three lovely billboards of Mary surrounded by children. When an extra sign was printed I took its center section and put Mary's smiling face over the McCain sign. Mary took his place in my front yard. She went on to regain her seat, one she had lost two years earlier in part because of a nasty whisper campaign.

To top off her re-election to the School Board, Mary was chosen to be the Board's new chairman. I wrote a Reader column called simply, "Mary," in January 2004. It was a post-campaign rebuttal to the the whisper campaign. It can still be found on my old website. Just Google: snowbizz.com, Diogenes, Mary.

Mary's sign was the perfect size to place on my newly leveled wine cave. I enjoyed the thought of keeping Mary captive there. The two of us had enjoyed tippling reds after school board meetings. To make it easy to get into my elevated entrance, I built a solid wooden ladder and a small door on a hinge. It was made out of another sign I'd once put in my yard complaining about a huge pot hole in front of our house. Public comment is my forte.

I always expected that Mary would come over some day so I could tease her about my cool floor. But the Red Plan intruded and we found ourselves on opposite sides. We've made up but she has never been over to see her smiling face. But my grandson saw it. And its true. Pretty Mary Cameron who, because she was black, never had a single date in her three years at Duluth's Central High School, does look a little like Michelle Obama. Especially when she flashes her million-dollar-smile.

So, no, I don't have Michelle Obama in my basement. It's my friend, Mary Cameron.

Everything that Harry writes that is not about the imminent destruction of Earth as we knew it is superfluous. But, he prattles on at: lincolndemocrat.com

THE PARTY OF GOD

Or the Party of the moneylenders?

Unlike Jesus, who turned people's minds to heaven and to being their brother's keeper, some people have sought power in politics and turned to the dark force which once tempted the son of man. Their reasoning: if its "Biblical" its OK. Thus we had slavery and its aftermath which continues today even on the most segregated day of the week, Sunday.

Graham Crackers

"America's Pastor," Billy Graham, with President Nixon, left. Billy's son, Franklin Graham, with President Trump, right

Long ago in a country far, far away, a young boy smitten by the love of God would become "America's Pastor" and the counselor of Presidents from Dwight David Eisenhower to Barack Obama. Then his son Franklin would do the same.

In the middle of that first pastor's years, my parents moved me to Minnesota and gave me three years without church or Sunday School. I didn't miss it. When I started high school they introduced me to congregationalism and a local pastor with liberal minded views. I felt at home in a "main stream" church. Many of their children had been going on freedom rides to the South. I was well along my journey to agnosticism and didn't mind mainline Christianity's MYOB attitude (mind your own beeswax) about faith. Unlike Billy Graham's Crusade, WASPY churches were no longer terribly evangelical.

But Billy Graham had his admirers. One of them was an inoffensive, if awkward, school mate of mine, Bixler Baker. One day Bixler made me an offer. He told me he had "free tickets" for a movie. The combination of Bixler and free tickets made me instantly skeptical. They were for a movie that the Billy Graham Crusade had just made to reach the millions of souls who had failed to troop into his football stadiums for a Graham revival. "Maybe," I replied diplomatically not wishing to hurt my friend's feelings. I wasn't remotely interested.

He pressed a "free" ticket in my hand with a look of saintly pleasure that made me feel terribly guilty. I knew he would ask me what I thought of the movie so I glumly walked over to the State theater. I endured the movie's proselytizing and *surprise, surprise* - a rebellious boy's flawed but earnest parents took him to a Graham Crusade where he surrendered to God's call. He was saved! I slunk out of the theater as speakers came to the stage welcoming viewers eager to repent.

Whatever I told Bixler about the movie afterward I know he was delighted. Thinking back on it, my ninety minutes of torment was an act of true charity - on my part.

Billy had been gracious about other Christian paths. America's pastor had hobnobbed with Presidents who were Quakers, Baptists, and Catholics. One of the Quakers was Richard Nixon and the relationship Billy and Dick had would come back to haunt Billy.

In 1994 Nixon's Chief of Staff HR Haldeman published a book that recounted how Nixon and Graham privately bad-mouthed Hollywood's Jewish community. Billy denied it vehemently. "Those are not my words," Graham said. "I have never talked publicly or privately about the Jewish people, including conversations with President Nixon, except in the most positive terms."

Eight year's later his cover was blown when the infamous Nixon tapes were made public. They were damning. "They're [the Jews] the ones putting out the pornographic stuff," Graham told Nixon. "The Jews stranglehold has got to be broken or the country's going down the drain," he continued.

Graham added that Jews did not know his true feelings about them. "I go and I keep friends with Mr. Rosenthal (A.M. Rosenthal) at The New York Times and people of that sort, you know. And all -- I mean, not all the Jews, but a lot of the Jews are great friends of mine, they swarm around me and are friendly to me because they know that I'm friendly with Israel. But they don't know how I really feel about what they are doing to this country."

To his credit, Graham admitted his shortcomings when they were exposed in 2002 and begged for forgiveness.

Billy's fourth child, Franklin, who has taken over his father's ministry has departed from his father in one significant way. Coming to his father's pulpit after the Moral Majority began making the GOP the party of God he joined them vociferously and abandoned his father's bipartisan ways.

It is apparent to me that Franklin Graham like his father is all too human. Of the lying-est president in history Franklin said last January, "I don't think the president [Trump] is sitting there behind the desk trying to make up lies. I don't believe that for a second. Has he misspoken on something? Sure. All of us do that. You do it and I do it. And sometimes we get the facts wrong and we say something that later on we realize, we could've said it better or it was misrepresented."

Franklin Graham should revisit the 8th chapter of John: ". . . If you abide in My word, you are My disciples indeed. [32] And you shall know the truth, and the truth shall make you free."

Christians are not immune from the truth

Cynthia Robinson told our fifth-grade teacher that I didn't want to join the science club. That was a lie and I didn't much like her. One day Cynthia heard me take the Lord's name in vain. She scolded me imperiously, telling me that God's would strike me dead. So, I looked up to heaven and called out, "God strike me dead!" At a momentary loss for words, Cynthia shrugged off her disappointment and told me, "Well, one day when you're not expecting it, God *will* strike you dead."

In seventh grade, now a Minnesotan, I was astonished to learn that my new Lutheran buddy didn't know how to play cards. His mother was shocked when she discovered I'd taught him how to play games like gin rummy, crazy eights and concentration. I assured her we were not gambling. That was true. My dad had given me a stern lecture on the subject when an older boy won a quarter from me on a dart throw. Years later, I discovered how deeply I had corrupted my new friends family when he told me his parents had joined a bridge club.

Some Christians can be a little myopic when they read, "The truth will set you free."

The Twenty-thousand-and-first lie

Thursday Nov. 12th, 2020

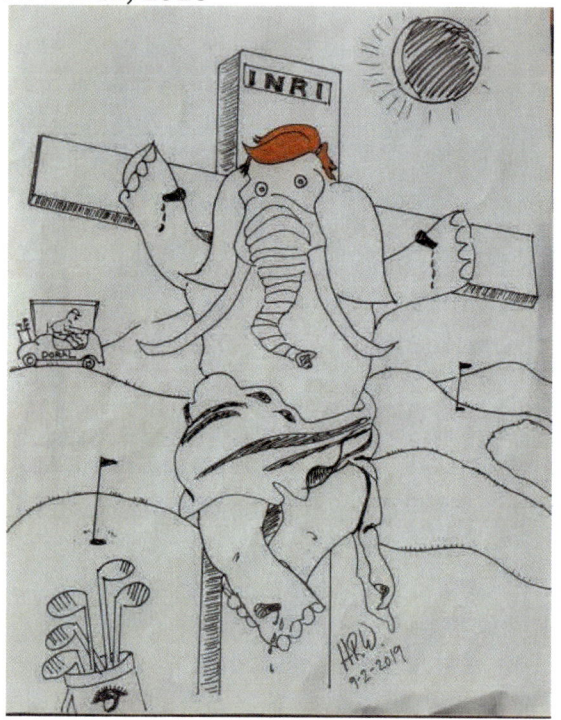

A yellow-headed Republican is a poor substitute for Jesus on the cross. Illustration by Harry Welty.

No, Mr. Trump. You did not win the election. America won. So far.

And as with other wars victory has come, is still coming, with great loss of life. The war you have waged for your reelection and against truth and science will have cost more lives by the time Joe Biden is sworn in than any war of combat in our nation's history. Your reelection campaign has been a crusade on behalf of those most loyal to the Trump fad especially evangelical voters.

Christian fads are nothing new. Before Christianity became Rome's state religion, some early Christians yearned to die in the Arena in an ostentatious display of martyrdom. Distressed church fathers tried unsuccessfully to discourage them.

Closer to our time, itinerant preachers would give such invigorating shows of hellfire piety in Indiana's backwoods that a very young Abe Lincoln would mimic their fervor to entertain his friends.

When my children were little, evangelicals ruined Halloween by calling trick or treating an act of Satan worship.

At the coming of the Millennium, evangelicals warned of the "Rapture," that would leave the Earth littered with the cast off clothing of the saved and a sorry lot of the damned who would be "Left Behind."

In my youth, preachers burned Beatles records across the South when John Lennon joked that the Beatles were more popular than Jesus. They were!

Today's preachers should be burning the Art of the Deal. Instead, they treat our reality show "billionaire" President as the epitome of their prosperity gospel. Now the rich can be sure of passing on to heaven, never mind the camels which are stuck in the eye of a needle.

Here's the truth that could set so many free - - Donald Trump is not the second coming of Christ. He is much more likely to be found in the Book of Revelation, if you know where to look.

For four years I've been afraid that America was a hair's breadth from succumbing to a demagogue. By a hair's breadth, those four years have come to an end.

A second Civil War will not happen. Farmland and city cannot be as easily sundered as two swaths of territory north and south of the Mason-Dixon Line.

There was no blood shed on election night 2020 despite Trump's encouragement.

He has been an incompetent dictator. Mitch McConnell-led Republicans are not incompetent. They have perfected all the political mechanics to tilt elections in their favor: gerrymandering, voter suppression, untraceable dark money and the iffy restraints of social networks.

To enforce their tinkering they have guaranteed 40 years of Republican packed courts.

And most troubling, after Trump new candidates will have a much longer leash to sell snake oil. 240 years of America's presidential succession is under threat here as it is in many nations that once followed the American example – the American experiment.

Until Alzheimer's overtakes me, I will not forget how silent the Republican party has been in the face of Donald Trump's violation of common decency, his narcissistic refusal to concede defeat, and his 20,000 lies.

I listened carefully to Joe Biden's speech after Pennsylvania's votes were assured. He spoke hopefully of our "Possibilities" which reminded me of Hubert H. Humphrey's definition of politics as "the art of the possible."

Biden drew on the popular religious anthem 'On Eagles Wings' to bear up America.

I liked what I heard. The following morning at our church's television worship I heard the lyrics to another hymn that America should keep in mind: "When I look into the face - of my enemy - I see my brother - I see my sister."

That's a New Testament message that evangelicals could and should champion. Or they could remember what Abraham Lincoln, the war President and founder of President

Trump's political party, said: "My concern is not whether God is on our side; my greatest concern is to be on God's side … "

My daughter recently learned that her 10-year-old son had stopped reciting the Pledge of Allegiance in School. Instead he stood in mute but respectful silence. After last week's election he confided that he could once again begin reciting it.

Like Lincoln, my grandson bears malice towards none.

Jesus said, "The truth will set you free."

Or to paraphrase a very American maxim, 'Fool me 20,000 times, shame on you. Fool me 20,001 times, shame on me!'

When not writing in his blog Harry Welty can be found standing in front of mirrors sticking his tongue out. Sometimes you can catch him doing it at: lincolndemocrat.com.

Le tables de la Loi

Thursday Nov. 24th, 2022

It snowed a couple days ago and I sculpted two simple tablets with the roman numerals 1-10 on them. Well, not quite. I made an amendment by omission.

In place of Roman numeral IX, the proscription against bearing false witness, I substituted a question mark. I wasn't quite finished with our 2022 midterm elections or the breaking of the ninth commandment by a President who said he was cheated out of victory – a president who has probably broken all of the other commandments as well.

The Bible says Moses brought God's commandments down from Sinai and that he broke the tablets they were carved on in a fury. He discovered that while he was communing with God, God's people had begun worshiping a golden idol reminiscent of Trump Tower. I think there is a message in this that Republicans and Trump supporters ought to take to heart.

Local Republicans may think this column is my upraised middle finger to them, their President and their party. But they are wrong about the finger.

The finger I raise, is Mr. Pointer. I imagine raising it like Moses. But maybe rather than Moses I'm just a schoolmarm wagging my finger at children who let a pig loose in the school.

For the past three years I've had the privilege of talking politics with a French pen pal. Like most Europeans she is well aware of America's pugnacious evangelicals.

The French soured on Christianity during their Revolution. The millions of deaths in two world wars just sped up the abandonment of the cathedrals. No one in France tries to put the commandments up in Hotel de Ville. What? I wondered, would my pal think of them. Of course, I sent her a picture of my snow tablets and did my best to explain them.

In turn my friend wondered whether her family would recognize the tables of Moses. She passed them on.

Her oldest daughter drew a blank writing back that the cat had got her tongue. However, daughter-in-law nailed it:

"These are the 10 commandments and the ninth is you will not lie (in short) something that Trump and the Republicans did not respect."

I wish my fellow Republicans understood that the word "liberal" is time honored. Many of our nation's favorite Republican presidents, starting with Abraham Lincoln, qualify as liberals.

Liberalism, springs from the New Testament. Jesus spells it out in Mathew 5, 1-12 in a passage called the "Beatitudes." If it's good enough for Jesus it ought to be good enough for Republicans.

"Blessed are the poor in spirit, for theirs is the kingdom of heaven. Blessed are those who mourn, for they will be comforted. Blessed are the meek, for they will inherit the earth. Blessed are those who hunger and thirst after righteousness, for they will be filled. Blessed are the merciful, for they shall be shown mercy. Blessed are the pure in heart, for they will see God. Blessed are the peacemakers, for they will be called the sons of God. Blessed are those who are persecuted because of righteousness, for theirs is the kingdom of heaven. Blessed are you when people insult you, persecute you and falsely say all kinds of evil against you because of me. Rejoice and be glad, because great is your reward in heaven, for in the same way they persecuted the prophets who were before you."

If this sounds like Democrats then Republicans should steal the page back from them.

While I was fussing over my sculpture a neighbor stopped his pickup out front, rolled down his window, and offered some friendly banter. We go back to opposite corners of a kinder and gentler Republicanism. His mother was a pro-life legislator.

As he sized up two suggestive curves in my front yard he asked me if I was treading on dangerous waters. I caught his drift and laughed.

I told him his question reminded me of an anecdote I'd read years ago in Readers Digest. It was in a section called "Life in these United States." There was a kid who was busy making a snowman in his front yard. It had two alarming protrusions projecting forward.

The boy's parents caught sight of it from their window and panicked. They summoned him inside and angrily demanded to know what he was doing.

Taken aback by their anger the boy stuttered "It's Jimmy. He's putting his hands on his head to keep his ears warm."

A big smile spread across my Republican friend's face. We need more smiles and fewer "shalt nots" to restore America.
Welty also shoots his mouth off at lincolndemocrat.com

A Christmas pageant
Dec. 28th, 2023

One of Claudia Welty's favorite children's books

I have been content to be apart from and a part of one particular church for 40-plus years. Many hundreds of its members have come and gone during that time. Several dozen have had their ashes interred in a garden beside the church which I occasionally water below windows whose casings I have painted from towering extension ladders.

Why an agnostic like me has remained a part of and apart from this church for so long, has many explanations. I will never forget the Easter morning 41 years ago after my daughter's birth when I sat in a packed church quietly enjoying my life-changing fatherhood, as my wife rested in the hospital. Nor will I forget my daughter's postponed baptism, when her grandmother died in a plane crash flying north to witness the sacrament.

Nor will I forget the children's time when our pastor asked the kids what they thought the pilgrims and Wampanoags ate for Thanksgiving and my daughter suggested, "bacon."

Several hundred Presbyterians chuckled in unison until my stricken daughter sprang up and cried in anguish, "They laughed at me!"

As she ran to her parents, she left several hundred guilt-stricken Presbyterians in her wake. We carried her outside the sanctuary where she said in a fury, "When I grow up I'm gonna wreck this church!"

Honestly, I can't think of a better string of episodes to keep a vigilant religious skeptic like me coming back for more.

Last Sunday's worship service was no exception. Our now threadbare congregation of gray and balding heads watched a Christmas spectacle, that would surely have astonished the strict Scots who founded Glen Avon Church on Oatmeal Hill. One week earlier, our free-thinking youth director promised us an interesting Christmas pageant.

I've been a patient observer of many such pageants before, some with children and some with the sturdy men of the church who for 80 years donned biblical garments to portray the Disciples sharing the light of a risen Christ in the hushed, candle-lit darkness of our sanctuary. As the disciples aged and began joining the host in the garden their dutiful but weary daughters grew tired of lugging out the cumbersome paraphernalia of the "Feast of Lights." Our Christmas programs became exclusively youth oriented with a cast of innocents.

Being orderly Presbyterians our programs never unraveled quite like the one described in my wife's favorite Xmas book, The (worst) BEST Christmas Pageant ever.

Last Sunday we tempted fate. I suspect our free thinker planted some subversive seeds of mischief in our youngest church members as her promised "improvisation" took shape. The improvisation began with the children, who were given charge of casting the manger tableau. The elders sitting in the pews were entreated to kindly don whatever costume a child offered them. The first to be cast was Mother Mary. A sky-blue scarf was entrusted to the small hands of gamins whose grandfather, son of a former church organist, plays percussion for our "Revelation" choir.

These gamins have brightened church services since they could stand, and discovered their grandfather's extra sticks which they used to bop along with him as he beat out a tempo. When they offered their grandfather Mary's sky-blue scarf a look, half of good sport and half of "why did I just play 'Yellow Submarine' to bar full of drunken Hell's Angels" crossed his face as he reluctantly walked to the manger.

All the little children grinned broadly at their ingenious casting. The role of Joseph was given to the statuesque mother who was once a local basketball great. Her even taller father, who shepherds many grandchildren every Sunday, was given donkey ears as he joined the animals in the stable.

Two white-haired grandmothers put on red hens-combs as they walked to the manger where they were given orange beaks to complete their barnyard ensemble. After the children had cast another two dozen congregants they noticed their Biblical raiments were running low. They realized that if they wanted to join the fun at the front of the church they'd better start putting on costumes before they were all gone. In short order all ages and manners of pilgrims were milling around the manger.

Casting was almost complete. Only one vital role was yet to be cast – Baby Jesus. To whom would the children offer swaddling cloths? Of course, they were given to the retired accountant not quite three times as old as the martyred Jesus. He wasn't really given swaddling cloths, otherwise he might not have made his way forward in such good humor. As he approached, the youth director assured him he need not climb into the cradle.

My daughter, who never did wreck the church, has two older boys. One of them played "Away in the Manger" with his grandmother in the chimes choir. His younger brother read a preamble that set the scene with practiced authority.

I, who remained seated, enjoyed it all very much but I don't think anyone enjoyed the pageant more than the many adults who on that Sunday found themselves transformed into wise men, shepherds and animals of the stable.

Welty often wakes up cheerfully at lincolndemocrat.com.

An Agnostic's Prayer with a prologue
7-5-2000 from www.snowbizz.com:

In the summer of 2000 I was a chaperone at Group Workcamp's "Royal Gorge Workcamp." It was the fifth Workcamp I've chaperoned in the last six years for Glen Avon Presbyterian Church's senior high school students. My daughter and or son have been participants for the last six years.

These have been wonderful experiences. Group Workcamps began in 1977 after a terrible flood in Colorado's Big Thompson Canyon. Organized to aid people after that flood, Group Workcamps now sponsors over 30 Workcamps across the United States and Canada each summer. I think there will be 46 camps next year. These camps organize church youth to repair and paint the homes of people who can't do this work for themselves. This year the camps will have hit a new milestone as their 100,000th work-camper begins his or her labors.

As an agnostic, I have had to ask myself how honest my participation in Workcamps is since they are tied to a Christian witness I can't fully embrace. The word "agnostic" is Greek and means to be without wisdom. Unlike Atheists, who actively deny the existence of a supreme being, I make no claims about the metaphysical or spiritual world.

Ironically, I have led evening devotions with the young men from our church at these Workcamps since I began attending them in 1995. I did so again this year.

One evening last week I was faced with a personal challenge which I could not easily resolve. I composed a prayer and hoped that a particular member of our group would listen closely. When our devotions concluded I ended with the prayer and explained that it was personal in nature and not meant to speak for the group. It was an act of confession to our young men as much as to God.

Here follows my prayer:

Dear God,

I am a fraud. When I pray to you I'm praying to an idea I have not accepted. I am not a member of your church although you see me there on many Sundays singing in your choir.

If you exist, as so many people in your church and my Glen Avon Presbyterian Church believe, you are certainly not surprised by my confession. You know that when I pray to you it is because   I can think of nothing more worthy than the acts of caring and humanity the belief in you inspires in others. And God, every time I pray I search my heart for the right words, for honest words. I do not believe in the void your absence would demand. That void, that anarchy, that confidence in personal gratification limited only by the whims of man I find repellent, worse yet, the source of evil, both petty and profound.

Perhaps God, I am not alone. Perhaps to one degree or another, your followers share similar doubts, which are revealed by their confessions. In every prayer worthy of the name, there is an element of confession. Each sin confessed testifies to personal rebellion against you and a denial of the path you have set before us.

Forgive this seeker, Lord, as you forgive those who, although they have found you, stray from your path.

Know that everyone in this workcamp, who labors for the humble and vulnerable people of Canon City, is struggling to stay on your path by their service to others.

Lord, forgive the frauds, forgive the sinners, and look kindly on all seekers.

Help us complete your good works, here at the Royal Gorge Workcamp.

HOT BUTTONS

Abraham Lincoln declined to say which side of the Civil War he thought God supported. Not so the Party of God. The *Party of God* is deeply allied with one side of these four hot buttons. Like Lincoln I can't speak for God. I simply offer my thoughts:

3 columns that exemplify my thinking about guns,
3 columns that exemplify my thinking on abortion
1 column that exemplifies my thinking on both gays and recreational drugs

Growing our hearts two sizes bigger might help us.

The Good Guys and Sheriff Tweet
May 21, 2020

In a show of support for the rights of front line medical professionals to live free or die, patriots armed with semi-automatics answered President Trump's tweet to liberate America's economy.

When my junior high buddy's Father gave him an air rifle he asked me to go with him to an NRA gun safety course. My parents who never owned a firearm more lethal than a squirt gun didn't mind. The police had once investigated them for attacking friends with squirt guns. There is only one conclusion to draw from that kind of governmental overreach. We need more lethal weapons to protect us from Big Brother.

Good guys recently overran Michigan's capital to protect us from Big Brother Fauci. They were answering the tweets from the "Chief law enforcement officer of the United States," (self proclaimed) Sheriff Trump. They brought their semi-automatics to warn the Governor that the Posse Comitatas is here to protect us from democracy, if necessary. The Posse has a storied history.

For ten years after the Civil War Federal troops were thinly spread over the defeated rebel states. Among their "peace keeping" duties they protected schools for black children for whom education had been outlawed under slave state laws. They also enforced constitutional amendments granting citizenship and voting rights to former slaves. In protecting the freedmen the troops were honoring fallen comrades whose blood had consecrated many a battlefield as the last full measure of their devotion to the Union. But, that's not how the defeated traitors saw it. Ex-confederates regarded the 13th, 14th and 15th amendments extending God's "unalienable" rights of equality to all men as an abomination when these rights were extended to their former property. Like today's sheltering-in-place, freeing slaves was ruinous to the South's economy. With so few Union soldiers it was easy for the Ku Klux Klan to put on bed sheets and burn, shoot and lynch freedmen foolish enough to think that their side had won the war.

To end this "Reconstruction" the South offered Republicans a deal after a controversial 1876 presidential election. If the North pulled its federal troops out the South they would let Republican Rutherford B Hayes claim victory over Democrat Sam Tilden. To make sure no American soldiers ever again stuck their bivouacs into the South they passed the Posse Comitatas Act. No more would military intervention be permitted to control civic disturbances in any state. Crowd control authority was given to local sheriffs who could keep order by forming posses. A generation of Baby Boomers in the Sixties might not have known about this statute but could see it in action every week. Boomers had about twenty TV westerns to choose from on television. They regularly saw TV sheriffs deputize posses to track down bank robbers, cattle rustlers and Indian gun runners.

By the 1990's the National Rifle Association had devolved from championing hunters to lobbying for gun manufacturers. Their ubiquitous bumper stickers read, "I'll give you my gun when you pry it from my cold dead hands." Boomers infatuated with posses decided they didn't need a sheriff. Like the Klansman of yore the posses comitatus protect America like turbaned jihadis carrying kalishnikovs through a middle eastern war zone. They became heavily armed survivalists ready to repel an attack from Red Dawn, aliens from outer space and liberals run amok. Damned liberals think that man-killing-machines ought to be licensed like a car.

So sacred is the gun to Second Amendment enthusiasts today that they shrug off 24,000 annual gun suicides and 14,000 homicides as a small price to pay. But those deaths pale compared to the deaths of 2 percent of the US population by corona virus. That would take out 6.6 million Americans. That's six times the number warriors who died in all of America's wars. Once part of the "Pro-life" Republican Party, gunslingers point their semiautomatics at public officials to warn them that corona virus deaths are a small price to pay for getting America back to work. Now its Dr. Fauci who is the NRA's mortal enemy, not "bad guys with guns."

At sixty-nine and long retired I'm economically expendable. I planned to live another thirty years to watch my grandchildren grow up but I'd sacrifice for them. But its not just me at risk. It turns out stray virus infected spit could kill my grandsons too despite their youth. And my wife had a pacemaker implanted after heart surgery a year ago. She has to take antibiotics for dental work. She's also vulnerable! The Posse wants me to sacrifice a helluva lot to reelect Sheriff Trump. And let's be honest. He's been a lousy Sheriff. For months while the virus got a jump on us he kept bragging about how he had it under control. Those big talking lies put my grandchildren, my wife, our doctors and nurses, our nursing home residents and staff in the jaws of death.

So, no thank you "good guys." Take off your grinning death masks and stop brandishing your goddamned semiautomatics. Put them back in your gun lockers. I'll take my chances with the bad guys.

Welty shoots his guns off at: www.lincolndemocrat.com

The Tears of Vyle Rittenhouse

Kyle Rittenhouse is a kid. The same kind of kid who, had he been shot down on the field of battle, could have cried out "Mommy" as life drained from his body. Such a death, tragic as it would have been, can certainly be called heroic.

But there was nothing noble, let alone heroic, about Kenosha. Kyle Rittenhouse was not answering the summons of his nation. He had his mom drive him across the state, where a friend was keeping his illegally purchased assault rifle so he could watch riots up close. He was not a cop. He was a moth. Worse, he was a self appointed vigilante, who didn't know jack shit. All he knew, or should have known, was what every bad guy who takes a loaded gun to a robbery knows. I learned it from an NRA gun class in junior high. Never point a gun, loaded or otherwise, at anybody....unless, like a bad guy, or a real cop, you mean to use it.

When a bad guy puts ammunition in a gun for a robbery its there for one purpose only. To be used if necessary. No matter how often he tells himself or a jury that he never meant to kill anybody a killer is still guilty as sin. This is why armed robbery, even without deaths, is judged so much more harshly than other crimes without weapons. Seventeen-year-old Kyle Rittenhouse went with his assault rifle prepared to kill someone. And he did. Two someones and nearly one other. But he got off.

Maybe he got off because of video evidence of his victims doing exactly what people can be expected to do when someone points a gun at them. But a lot of black Americans are not stupid to note that a white state acquitted a white kid recklessly carrying a loaded rifle where he had no right to be.

Its hard to forget Kyle's reaction when faced with a prosecutor determined to give the boy a man's prison sentence. Under a withering examination the boy, confident in his virtue, even smug based on pre-trial activities, burst out in contorted howls and sniffles like the child he was while he asserted his innocence.

Juvenile offenders are usually treated as children but in many states children who kill are treated like adults, especially in the Republican states of the South. Especially if the accused are black. Southern courts have been so rabid for swift justice that in recent years their prisons have had to release a great many innocent men convicted because undiscovered or suppressed evidence sent them to a life behind bars. Now Kyle faced this possibility, if found guilty. But of course, he wasn't. What the jury decided will have ripples across the nation.

There is a case with similar issues in a Georgia State Court. Three men, afraid that a black man jogging down a suburban street had committed a property crime, took on Rittenhouse-like police powers, set up a pickup truck barricade and chased him into the rifles they leveled at him with another pickup truck. Kyle Rittenhouse, said he feared that men running towards him would take the loaded weapon he brought and use it against him. That is now the defense of the men who shot jogger, black jogger, Ahmaud Abery to death. They maintain that having surprised the jogger and cornered him there was only one rational response. Shoot the nigger. And that's what they called Mr. Abery. "Nigger."

But its not racism on trial in these courtrooms. Its an expansion of the novel new idea of stand-your-ground laws. Put a loaded gun in someone's face and if you think they might grab it from you stand your ground with bullets. Its a fantastic new freedom for vigilantes like the ones who plotted the kidnapping of the Michigan Governor because they didn't like how she was trying to stop the spread of Corona-virus. One of them has been sentenced to six years. But if future vigilantes don't go around plotting to kidnap politicians, they are good to go. They just have to chase them into their loaded assault rifles.

All of this is not a tragedy for the talking heads of Fox News. Its red meat. Rush Limbaugh wannabe Tucker Carlson has invited the recently acquitted Rittenhouse to receive Fox News's equivalent of a ticker tape parade down New York City's Fifth Avenue. (Just where Donald Trump said he could shoot somebody and get away with it.)

Kyle will be getting a big pat on the back for citizenship on prime time Fox. It might even have been Tucker Carlson who blew the dog whistle that led Kyle Rittenhouse to Kenosha and prompted him to take up arms. Golly, these multi-millionaire Fox megaphones for civil war just keep getting richer every day.

That's Vyle Rittenhouse for you.

Everything that Harry writes that is not about the imminent destruction of Earth as we knew it is superfluous. But, he does prattle on at: www.lincolndemocrat.com

Our Better Angels
Dec 20, 2020

Six years ago I made the only snow sculpture that made me cry. Judging by comments on various websites, which posted this photo, I was not the only one so affected. The sculpture was of an angel wrapping her arms around children after the Sandy Hook Massacre.

Shooting the innocent has become an ever more oppressive way for the angry, depressed, and suicidal to share their suffering. There have always been other methods of inflicting pain but the gun offers advantages over torches, poisons and sharp blades. These advantages advance exponentially with ever more impressive engineering. I've just read a news story about the US military's excitement at the prospect of a new battleground rifle that will expel rounds with so much force that Kevlar will be no more of an impediment than a rag. I'm sure the National Rifle Association looks forward to defending its membership's rights once this weapon finds its way into civilian hands. The Bill of Rights is, as it goes without saying, sacred.

So much of the Republican gospel is sacred that it is above compromise, except when it's abandoned.....like Free Trade. I've never been quite sure which codicil to the Bible makes firearms so special. When the Constitution was adopted by the American people there was no assembly line production of guns. Ammunition had yet to be rifled for accuracy and lead shot had to be melted by the gun owners themselves to fit their eccentric barrels. There was no rapid fire. Instead, ranks of European trained soldiers stood in line to fire into opposing lines of soldiers. That way their wild shots could hit the broad side of a barn. How frustrating for the British that the Americans adopted "Indian" tactics and hid behind trees to shoot back.

To curtail our "excessive" current gun laws there is an NRA chorus calling for the arming of teachers. This would help, I guess, when some gun toting villain blasts his or her way past the glass security doors, like those now found in Duluth's Red Plan schools. Perhaps the NRA could go a step further and pay for gun safes in our classrooms so that our children could fight back when faced with a semi or fully automatic rifle. Right now Duluth's kids are being trained to throw things, *anything*, at bad guys who poke a gun into their classrooms. That's one way to throw the book at a bad guy.

I have long been confounded at the gun lobby's rationale for letting Americans buy guns on the sly to avoid red tape. But you can't sell a car without transferring the title! Why should a gun designed and capable of taking out a Las Vegas concert crowd be any different?

In 1994, twenty years before Sandy Hook, I wrote a letter to the News Tribune as a fledgling politico endorsing gun control. It wasn't my best. I wrote about a "slavish" devotion to the Constitution when I should instead have suggested that enforcement of the Bill of Rights should be fluid and flexible. Guns today are not like those of the sparsely populated and lightly armed America of 1794. And back then, the Federal Government wasn't a wimp when it came to law enforcement. *President* George Washington took to horseback to command an American Army enforcing tax collection and to crush Pennsylvania's "Whiskey Rebellion. "

I don't recall what prompted me to write that letter in 1994 even though the subject bad been on my mind for a long time. Back then, I was upset that America's inner cities were riddled with black on black gun violence. I felt, perhaps naively, that reducing the production of cheap handguns would have a salutary effect. But it might have been another recent act of violence that stirred me to share my opinion. For 1994 was also the year that a School Board member's sister was shot to death at her own front door when her husband, or ex, came to revenge his family's dissolution.

Joan Peterson has done what I hope I would have done. She's made passing sensible gun control her personal ministry. I was impressed to read that Joan encouraged Joe Radinovich, the Democrat's candidate for Minnesota's 8th Congressional seat, to open up about a similar tragedy in his life. Telling that story turned Joe Radinovich's campaign around and helped him climb out of polling hell to surge to within five points of catching the eventual winner of that race.

Unsurprisingly, the election was followed by more senseless deaths including a massacre of innocents at a Pennsylvania synagogue. I saw Joan at a vigil honoring the innocents soon afterwards. In fact, there were three of us former school board members at this or another more formal vigil at Duluth's Temple Israel. The three of us have long been at odds over school district issues but Joan Peterson, George Balach and I were united on these occasions by the conviction that compromise would well serve America. It would also honor the sanctity of lives senselessly snuffed out in a fit of bile. PS. The letter writer who picked holes in my pro-gun control position 25 years ago was none other than the Reader's, Bill Rees, who has regularly fenced with Gary Burt on the Reader's opinion pages for years.

Harry Welty is a local eccentric and perennial candidate for office in Duluth who also pontificates on his blog: www.lincolndemocrat.com.

Sympathy for a Mass Murderer
Published April 20, 2002

I am a mass murderer. Now mind you, I'm not talking about just any old, garden variety, mass murder but the world's most massive holocaust ever. My crime is so vast that it dwarfs the Nazi death camps, the Soviet purges, and the atrocities of the Khmer Rouge all rolled into one. Though not pointing at me specifically; that's what Justin Krych said when he announced his candidacy for the State Senate at the 7th Senate District's Republican Convention two weeks ago. He was talking about abortion.

During his speech I sat next to my very good friend, Edith, a retired linguistics professor who, at age 84, is a fellow mass murderer. Had Edith and I attended the DFL convention, where every imaginable coalition becomes a "sub-caucus" we would probably have called ours the "mass murder sub-caucus." I noticed that Edith didn't applaud when Justin finished his speech. I didn't either.

Edith and I are remnants of an earlier era when the Republican Party had a more forgiving view of civil liberties and believed that government should mind its own business. For the past fifteen years Edith and I have clung to this philosophy. We are an extreme minority in the GOP though a comfortable majority in the general population.

Despite being mass murderers Edith and I are treated patiently, even cordially, by the pro-life majority, which simply hopes against hope that our better angels will eventually prevail. It's the "Hate the sin, love the sinner" ethos at its best. I suspect, however, that this patience could wear thin if the pro-choice forces ever threatened to become as common in the Party as they are in the general public.

After thirty years in the Party I can look on Justin's apocalyptic pronouncements with some equanimity. I too have been troubled by the idea of 'abortion on demand.' Minnesota's pro-choice association NARAL only lists me as "mixed" in my support of abortion rights. But I have always taken exception to the notion that anything in utero is the equal of my mother, wife, son or daughter, which happens to be the extreme position of the pro-life movement.

These views first took root in me in 1968 when I was a junior in high school. Back then pregnancy was looked upon as proper retribution for a single girl's sin. I'll never forget the waitress who lectured me when she overheard me discussing the subject. She told me that as far as she was concerned "if you're gonna play you gotta pay." In other words defenseless infants were to be their mother's wardens. This wasn't my idea of a loving mother/child relationship. This punitive approach was never really popular with the public and the pro-life movement didn't catch hold until it changed its focus to sympathy for the fetus. The issue of shame, however, has never really disappeared. It just went underground.

In my junior year of high school, I asked friends what had happened to the pretty girl that I'd developed a secret crush on as a sophomore. In hushed tones they told me that she had gotten pregnant. The father was a tall, good-looking, baby faced fellow, with a perpetual smirk on his face.

Being a single mother is not a very good option today for most women. Being a single mother in 1968 wasn't an option at all. In fact, being pregnant and unmarried was so shameful that tens of thousands of desperate young women, who had succumbed to the demands of smirking young men, were driven to back alley abortionists.

Today, "pro-life" advocates use photos of dismembered babies to make their case against abortion. Back in 1968 "pro-choice" supporters passed around crime scene photos of dead women, victims of botched abortions, blood trailing from their midsections, to win sympathy for the choice movement. Given the choice of a holocaust against the unborn or their mothers, I made an irrevocable decision and have never regretted choosing the mothers.

I like Justin Krych. A few weeks before the convention

I heard that he was eyeing the same legislative seat that I was interested in so I invited him out for lunch.

Justin is an eager, earnest, and respectful young fellow. We traded URL's for our websites. Justin had already visited my heretical site and was probably well aware of my pro-choice sentiments. I suspect that he'd already made the calculation that he could win an endorsement over me in a party convention given my beliefs.

Justin allowed as how he'd defer to the wishes of a nominating convention. In other words, if the GOP saw fit to endorse me over him because of my "electability" he would not oppose me. To win Justin's active support, however, I would have to abide by the platform about which I have serious reservations.

Without the Party's endorsement I would be required to appeal to the voters in a primary election. I think I know what the average voter thinks but I can't be sure that the average voter will feel compelled to vote in a primary let alone, a *Republican* primary.

I am left to ponder a simple question. Can the public have any sympathy for a mass murderer?

Welty is a small time politician who lets it all hang out at: www.snowbizz.com

The Aborted Girl
Published Apr 27, 2006

In 1990 I was ecstatic when the popular Republican State Auditor, Arne Carlson replaced the opportunistic, "pro-life," political hack who had defeated him in the gubernatorial primary with the help of naive religious conservatives. When John Grunseth was outed for having chased his daughter's friend around the family pool in a drunken attempt to rip off her bikini top he became instant poison. The pro-life Republicans had no face-saving choice other than to relinquish their death grip on the nomination in favor of Carlson. It would not be the last time that a false friend of religious conservatives would betray them.

The desire for revenge smoldered in the hearts of the pro-lifers as Governor Carlson's popularity soared. Four years later they were determined to oust him and nominated one of their own. Allen Quist, a very conservative legislator and his politically militant wife were a dynamic duo. Ms. Quist, an ex woman's libber, had come to see the error of her ways after her own abortion. She was determined to prevent other women from following her example. Wrapped as she was in a movement which told her she had murdered her child but whose repentance had assured her forgiveness, she took up her husband's cause. Hell hath no fury like a woman burdened by the guilt poured into her by her church.

To say I was paranoid about the religious right is an understatement. I viewed them the same way that the hero in Invasion of the Body Snatchers, viewed his neighbors whose bodies had been taken over by aliens. A few years earlier, in 1988, the "Christian businessman" Pat Robertson ran for the Republican Presidential nomination with the aid of a huge network of conservative churches. His followers were told to hide the fact that they were Christian conservatives, so that they could take over the Republican machinery. The only thing that had changed by 1994 was that they no longer had to hide their true intentions.

On a spring day that year, as a new set of Republican conventions were starting up, I took my daughter to Denfeld High School for an academic competition. While there I was introduced to one of the new pro-life refugees from the Democratic Party who were swelling the ranks of the GOP. He was eagerly telling a friend about a wonderful pro-life meeting that he'd just attended. A young woman had spoken to the gathering but not just any young woman. This young women's mother had tried to abort her but the child had survived the ordeal to give witness to it.

Although the story was being told to someone else I suspected it was being told for my benefit since I was one of the few remaining abortion rights supporters left in the Party. The story and the relish with which it was being passed along left me feeling isolated. How could I possibly defend myself against the witness of an aborted girl?

Then I met the young lady. She came to our first Arne Carlson campaign meeting. She didn't even look like the rest of us. She was wearing a modest cloth covering over her hair which I would have expected to see on an Amish or Mennonite woman but not a Carlson supporter. It practically screamed out, "I am a spy for the Quist campaign." As the only person there who knew about her witnessing background I kept my mouth shut and remained "Minnesota Nice." People are always innocent until proven otherwise.

A few days later I invited her over for a chat to determine her intentions. I'd never tried to unmask a secret agent before. Neither had I ever met anyone who had survived a third trimester abortion. To my surprise and delight she really turned out to be a supporter of Governor Carlson.

Soon to be married her dream was to do social work in the slums of a big city. She was conservative, but she also thought for herself. In fact, she was a very thoughtful person. Yes, she had given witness about her background but that experience seemed only to give her great compassion for women bearing a child that they could not care for.

She told me a most remarkable thing. She had once passed the Women's Health Center in Duluth which is infamous among pro-lifers for being one of the few locations in the Upper Midwest to offer abortion services. When she saw the tenacious Wisconsin man who regularly picketed the Health Center she had told him, maybe even yelled at him, that he shouldn't harass the miserable women who needed the Center's help.

For all I know, this remarkable young woman may have changed her mind since I met her. Perhaps she now pines for the day that the Supreme Court will reverse Roe vs. Wade. All that I can be sure of is that for a brief moment that summer, a young woman who was the survivor of a botched, saline abortion had the grit and the humanity to empathize with the desperate women who were resorting to the same cruel procedure which nearly ended her own life.

And she was on my side.

Welty is a small time politician who lets it all hang out at: www.lincolndemocrat.com

The Texas Christian Abortion Rangers

Thursday Sep. 9th, 2021

When Mao-Zedong decreed that no Chinese family could have more than one child he created a spy network in every city neighborhood and rural hamlet. It was composed of women with sensitive noses who could smell it when a women with a child missed her period.

With the help of the state they had a hundred ways to ferret out the truth. Guilty mothers-to-be, were handed to the nearest abortionist to keep China's population from exploding. You'd have thought they were illegal immigrants in America.

Today something similar to Mao's police state is unfolding in Texas. The Republicans ten gallon hat club has deputized Texans to poke through their neighbor's lives for pregnant women just like Mao's spy network. And better armed Texans can collect bounties for tracking them down.

The brainchild behind the law establishing this spy network is Mark Crutcher of "Spies for life." He's on the Internet at lifedynamics.com; with a list of the "most wanted" abortionists. He's been building an army for years.

One spy he groomed is James O'Keefe. O'Keefe's greatest triumph, back in 2010, was to send fake reporters into a local office of an organization that had been registering poor and black citizens to vote for 40 years. O'Keefe fiddled with his videos, which led to the closing of every ACORN office across the Country. Could Planned Parenthood be far behind?

Crucher's Texas Law offers a reward of at least $10,000 to any evangelical bounty-hunter who catches a doctor, nurse, mother, father, brother, sister, neighbor, minister or Uber driver that helped a woman get an abortion after her sixth week of pregnancy.

This is 18 weeks short of Roe v. Wade's constitutional waiting period. What's more, the law stacks the deck to insure that those accused of helping pregnant women can't effectively defend themselves.

If the vigilantes' case is brought to a court with justices like the ones Donald Trump appointed to the Supreme Court there is no limit on the fine. Its as high as the Texas sky.

The Texas law is intended to bankrupt abortion supporters so a million dollar fine for helping a desperate young woman is in the cards.

It reminds me of the Fugitive Slave law. And there is no exception even when the 'sperm donor' is Uncle Dick, a stepdad, the boyfriend who wouldn't take "NO" for an answer, or a stranger slipping drugs into a drink.

Constitutional protections notwithstanding, abortions like voting rights in Texas, are subject to armed Christian vigilantes who can also patrol black Texas neighborhood voting sites.

Crucher is now connecting bounty hunters to the internet to better track pregnancies. Facial recognition, black ops, email theft or hacking pharmacy records may not be far off.

Holy causes justify their means, and other states, particularly those adverse to masking, are drawing up their own versions of abortion bounty hunting laws.

It's as though Texas Republicans are repudiating Texas-born President, Lyndon Johnson for passing civil and voting rights laws for Black Americans and Texas's role in passing Roe v Wade on to the Supreme Court.

The considerable gravity of our second-most populous state shows clearly on maps of the states near its orbit. They were slave states; members of the Confederacy; passed Black codes to reinstate a slave-like non slavery; segregated schools; suppressed black voters; resisted masks and vaccines; saw an explosion of Covid 19 and, of course, voted for Trump.

Texas is firmly part of the South that fought the Declaration of Independence's proclamation that: "All men are created equal."

As far as Texas is concerned, pregnant women need not apply either.

Who are these Texans? They are God's people in all or mostly, white churches. Anyone who tells you that religion and politics don't mix doesn't know their history. When Iran's Ayatollahs took over Iran, they were intent on eradicating minority religions. But they were confounded by a Muslim law that forbade the execution of virgin girls. But like Texas Republicans they found a simple work around. If somehow the girls were raped executions could follow.

I was old enough to get a girl pregnant eight years before the Supreme Court put an end to the "back alley" abortions that took the lives of thousands of unhappy women. Women like my Mother lived those years when sex wasn't just taboo, it could mean death. Before the Roe vs. Wade era the coat hanger was the deeply personal symbol of religious oppression. Texas wants it back.

The bloody irony of the evangelicals is their alliance with the Republican Party which prefers to keep the taxes of the increasingly super rich low by the denying poor and unwanted children the homes, education and security those taxes could provide. That's socialism, a system that works well for all our European allies and their citizens and which evangelicals must avoid at all costs.

The old feminist pro-choice rally cry was "Its my body!" Today its the rallying cry of the Texas Christian Abortion Rangers.

Harry Welty thinks for himself at lincolndemocrat.com.

Stoning the Premier Danseur
Thursday Dec. 9th, 2021

Alexandra Danilova and Frederic Franklin, 1948

In the summer of 1971, just shy of 21, I moved to Washington D.C. to work as an intern for a Republican Congressmen. I wrote a modest report about the experience and got college credit for the work.

However, some of the best education I got never made it to my report.

I rented a room in a slummy townhouse a mile from the House Office Buildings. The young mail sorters on "The Hill" who lived there needed other tenants to sublet. Across the street lived a heavyset woman with a passel of children, one of whom I caught starting a fire in our alley. To our right was an elderly Jewish woman. After I bought a cake mix she was the first person I asked to lend me a cake pan. When she didn't have one I tried the door to our left.

Mark answered the door. Cordial and effeminate, he invited me in and hurriedly fetched a pan from his kitchen. We chatted a bit and I learned he taught at Catholic University.

After I went home to bake my cake I asked one of the mail sorters if he thought his neighbors were gay. To his credit he told me it was none of his business.

When I returned the pan Mark invited me in again and introduced me to Paul, co-owner of the townhouse. He taught at Georgetown University. They were beginning the gentrification of the Capitol's seedy Northeast.

Paul and Mark gave me a quick tour of their ground floor and asked me if I'd like to have a martini on their secluded patio. I could choke down beer, so I was game.

We had a pleasant conversation as I drank my first martini. It's funny how a special occasion can make sipping even an unpalatable drink rather nice.

I got a further surprise when they brought out a tray of ripe sliced tomatoes, lightly salted. I had detested USDA stewed tomatoes since school lunch in first grade but these were a revelation.

The three of us chatted for several genial hours and I enjoyed telling them about remote Kansas and Minnesota in America's far off nowhere.

Later that summer I was invited to a small soiree they were hosting. I suspected that I would be the odd man out. New York's Stonewall Riot two years before had demonstrated that some brave gays, when faced with enough police harassment, were quite capable of owning up to being different but, as is still the case, etiquette discouraged introductions by sexual preference.

As for me, I was strictly adhering to the ask-no-questions format. The gentlemen I was introduced to were witty and urbane. I was the youngest by 12-15 years.

The most senior guest was Freddie, then age 55, who was older than my parents by a similar stretch.

Wikipedia makes clear what I did not know then. He was famous. The other guests encouraged him to regale me with stories about the "ballerinas" he danced with in Paris. They were delighted to hear yet again how the girls considered it good luck to sleep with a virgin. Their take on the joke was not lost on me. Silly girls!

Two years later I would find a feature article in "the Minneapolis Star Tribune" about Mr. Franklin's storied past when he helped stage ballets in St. Paul with his perfect memory for choreography. Twenty years later I would ask my daughter's ballet teacher if she had heard of Franklin. Yes, she confirmed, he was a big deal.

Frederic Franklin's 2013 obituary in the "Washington Post" makes this clear. Between the sources I checked, his professional career began with America's own banana-belted Josephine Baker, whose dancers, however talented, were not ballerinas.

He went on to become the premier danseur for two decades at the Ballets Russe in what would become German-occupied Monaco.

That night our conversation swung to the young fellow's area of expertise, marijuana. My advocacy for the drug began the year before college when Newsweek explained that the drug sweeping college campuses was far less dangerous than alcohol. (Fifty years on, experience and science have modified this early impression.)

My offer to retrieve a lid from my house next door was met with enthusiasm, despite Mr. Franklin's expression of concern, which was roundly pooh-poohed by the others, including, I think, the New Yorker he was partnered with for the last 48 years of his life.

Certainly its downsides paled compared to living in Vichy, France, let alone admitting to homosexuality.

We passed a joint around and I, being the expert, took the deepest drag and was thus first to fall under the drug's charm as well as its chief peril – paranoia.

Suddenly, the roomful of arty sophisticates seemed less innocent. I was the party's ingenue but under-the-influence I was now a stoned ingenue. Being ingenious was no longer quite so cool.

Mark, who was sitting next to me, picked up his house cat and began petting it as though it were a munchie. A few stokes later his aim fell off and my thigh caught a couple strokes. I was in the wrong place and in no good condition to stay there. I left abruptly with what I've always feared was a curt expression of regret that my more sober-sided self would never have uttered. It was my last contact with the Director of Washington's Ballet Company.

Before I returned to Minnesota my neighbors invited me to house-sit the next summer as they traveled overseas. I was sorely tempted but wanted to think on it a bit (check with my parents).

I told my Dad I was pretty sure they were gay and he strongly discouraged me from putting myself at risk should their friends drop by. All six-foot-two of me thought that was a preposterous worry. Instead, I became a Republican in the summer of 1972, but that's another story.

Mr. Franklin survived AIDs and lived to the ripe old age of 98, according to his obituary. It didn't mention the soon-to-be college Republican who gave him his first puff of weed or the luck hungry girls of 1930s France. I'm glad they left me something to add to Freddie's biography.

Harry writes at lincolndemocrat.com.

GOD BLESS ANNE FRANK
AND THOSE WHO SUFFER
THROUGH NO FAULT OF THEIR OWN

I wrote my first column objecting to Israel's tempting fate by flexing its muscles instead of its brains in "Eve of Destruction" on May 17 2002.

Here are selections of three more recent columns expressing my frustration anew. I begin with the first three paragraphs from **"Which is the worst death?"** published Dec. 14, 2023:

One. You are a woman and after an unexpected hail of bullets at the music festival where you have been dancing, 10 sweaty men with NRA-approved rifles grab you, strip off your dress and take turns forcing their manhood into you for what seems an eternity as panic, excruciating pain and humiliation dull your mind followed by a bullet to your head at which point the burning of your body is no longer your concern.

Or Two: You are a mother holding an infant knowing retribution is coming from your heavily armed neighbors because a thousand "warriors" raped and murdered the neighbors in your name without your permission. When your apartment building is bombed you and your child plummet amid bricks, dust and shards of death and land in choking darkness under 20 feet of debris muffling your screams as you and the child at your breast succumb over days leaving you to pray that you and your child will meet again in heaven.

If you think a Democrat or a Republican has the right answer to this question shame on you. You are part of the tragedy of today's America.

Then there is this...

Let them eat grass

Thursday Oct. 19th, 2023

NOTE: What follows was largely composed before today's news that a million Palestinians have been ordered to leave their high-rises and apartments in Gaza City so that the Israeli air force can bomb their homes.

The baby shooting - soldier decapitating attack on the secular Jewish enemies of Israel's Prime Minister Benjamin "Bibi" Netanyahu may require 100 years to be viewed objectively. So, I will put myself in the shoes of missionaries to the Indians during the Indian wars of a past century. Distance allows more objectively.

In 1862 Sioux Indians, cheated out of their lands by Indian agents were now dependant on shipments of food promised to them in exchange for their lands. It was already stored next to their encampments. Asked for food one trader told the Sioux to "eat the grass." The Sioux went a little Hamas on white settlers.

Missionaries bringing the light of God to the Indians knew all about this perfidy. They were hard pressed not to sympathize with the "bad" Indians. But in 1862 there was only one acceptable response for most whites. It was almost universal and bore little resemblance to the New Testament.

Young warriors who saw their sisters, brothers mothers, wives and children starving did not have their elder's patience.

Their elders had been invited east to meet the Great White Father and more importantly been given sightseeing tours of America's wealth, power and population. The Sioux's ten or twenty thousand were pitted against tens of millions. To the young warriors, blind with rage, a different calculus applied. They saw Americans fighting a civil war. It gave them unfounded hope that they had a free hand to win back their lives.

It is said the first blood was drawn when an angry farmer accused hungry men of thievery for holding a single hen's egg. White retribution was now certain so they attacked other lonely cabins. The elders lost the debate. There was no turning back.

But even in 1862 thinly settled Minnesota had three times as many settlers as Sioux. A settler army would be fighting hungry men saddled with women and children. In 1862 starvation was not an acceptable justification for the excesses of the warpath. When the Sioux were defeated there was more starvation, concentration camps, typhoid, a new trail of tears and eventually the seizing of children for schools to erase Indian custom and language.

With the cool detachment of a hundred years it is easy to see how regrettable these unforgiving punishments were. But we moderns can comfort ourselves that we didn't do it. Minnesotans bent on the law, if not justice, ordered hasty military trials. They found 300 Sioux guilty of war crimes and sentenced them to be hung. The sentences were forwarded to the President for his review as Commander of the Army. Any other President would have likely hung them outright but despite the all consuming gravity of the North's faltering war effort Lincoln picked through the evidence and whittled the death sentences down to 39.

Today there is an almost irresistible call for vengeance against Hamas but it should be remembered that of 5 million Gazans only a few thousand swarmed and killed. That leaves a lot of innocents.

Similar stark calls for vengeance have decimated Syria, Iraq, Afghanistan, Venezuela and rained refugees. Some have skipped past Europe and traveled north from Panama to the Texas border. They face Narcos, Rapists, extortionists and tropical disease for a muddy slum under Mexican tents. No doubt tens of thousands of displaced Palestinians will soon join the trek.

The inhumanity of Hamas mirrors that of Iran. When the ayatollahs took over Iran they reminded their avenging angels that Islam forbade the execution of virgins but wink winked. Rape ends virginity.

One of my guides to the Mideast is my Minnesota contemporary NY Times columnist Tom Friedman. Fifty years ago while Christian schoolmates threw pennies on the floor for the greedy Jew to pick up he exalted when Israel beat back a surprise attack on three fronts. The Yom Kippur War proved Jews could hold their own.

He wrote From Beirut to Jerusalem in 1989. He was hopeful then and I've followed him since. His hope is fading but not his keen insight. Of this twisted massacre he points out that it wasn't observant land stealing Jewish settlers that Hamas attacked. Hamas targeted secular Israelis who are more sympathetic to Palestinians rights and who have repeatedly filled the streets to denounce Bibi.

What Hamas wants is for Israel to fail. They have decided that the best way to achieve failure is to strengthen the Prime Minister who has put staying out of jail ahead of preserving Israel's democracy. In this Bibi is not unlike Donald Trump who tried to achieve this on Jan 6th, 2021. Like the despots of Russia and China these "democratic" leaders are trying to pull a Napoleon and crown themselves Emperor. Benjamin Netanyahu may be remembered in a future century like the Indian Agent who told the Sioux to eat the grass.

Harry's words flow semi-regularly like Old faithful at lincolndemocrat.com

And finally there is this:

You have my sympathy Ilhan

Friday Feb. 15th, 2019

Prologue:

Ilhan Omar, Minnesota's new Islamic Congresswoman, has offered her "unequivocal" apology for twitting the fiercely pro-Israel Political Action Committee (AIPAC) in a tweet. Some of her fellow Congressmen are not satisfied. Full abasement is called for and perhaps congressional censure. Nevermind that traditional Republican condemnation of "Hollywood" for unraveling our moral fabric echoes similar calls from earlier politicians that paired amoral Hollywood with the slur "Jew-controlled."

Three years ago, I submitted the following column after accompanying a peace studies class to the Holy land. I suggested that it be the first of several to follow covering my two-week tour of Israel and Palestine. I'd grouse about how the reputedly corrupt Prime Minister Netanyahu insulted President Obama. I'd gasp about the belligerent drunk who hectored my liberal Jewish guides. I'd describe how I wept at Yad Vashem, as an archival movie showed two small shivering brothers sitting on curb in Warsaw, the little one listless and near death; both boys the age and image of my grandsons. The Reader didn't get back to me back then, so I resubmit the column today, to register my own impatience with the one-sided debate allowed in today's America, over an issue almost as important as guns, gays and gynecology.

Harry Welty's Holy Land Haj, Part 1

Photo credit Harry Welty. Subject: Moayyad Awni Jabarin

Most everyone could benefit from a spiritual journey even an agnostic like me. So, when my better half asked me last summer, if I'd like to travel with her seminary to study Israeli peace-making efforts it only took me a day to agree. Our departure in January, would necessitate my absence from the organizational meeting of the Duluth School Board. That would leave me with no say in the new leadership of a Board which had censured me the previous Christmas. It took Twenty-four hours for the quest for peace to take precedence over the quest for influence. I would tell my friends that if I could find peace in the most contested landscape on Earth I'd bring some of it back with me.

Friends shared their fears with me before I left. Piffle. Everywhere I passed, I found squads of Israeli soldiers with Uzis at their side or slung over their backs. Some of the pony-tailed warriors packing heat looked like the girls I dated in high school except that they wore khaki's and berets instead of strapless gowns. My trip was bookended by two remarkable coincidences. They are a fitting introduction to the installments I mean to share in coming weeks.

On our second night in Israel, outside the walls of Old Jerusalem, Claudia and I had a free night to dine by ourselves. We chose the posh Rooftop restaurant atop the Mamilla Hotel. Our DK guide gave it three dollar signs We had just returned from a Shabbat service at an orthodox synagogue. The stunning views of Jerusalem in the open terrace had to be viewed through a saran wrap shield that protected us from Israel's winter chill.

We were seated by a voluble American who made stinging comments about the naivety of peace advocates like those we had traveled with to Israel.

A sommelier brought us an excellent Israeli cabernet as two more tables were seated. The first was a party of four who took a long table with empty chairs for late arrivals. They were followed by a young couple who were shown to a table by our side. The pair held hands across the table and gazed dreamily into each other's eyes.

As we finished our meal an approaching hubbub caught my attention. I calmly told Claudia that the Prime Minister of Israel was headed our way. Claudia told me she didn't know what he looked like but I recognized him. I've been paying close attention to Bibi Netanyahu since the days of the first President Bush. The young man seated next to us turned toward us and explained, "I didn't vote for him." His girl friend's eyes pled with him to please shut up as a guard with a holstered gun under his North Face jacket stood with his back towards the disgruntled voter's chair. Another guard took position on the far side of the table with the extra chairs. The Prime Minister and his wife had finally arrived. More security fanned out onto the balcony just outside our saran wrap cocoon. I had purchased an identical North Face jacket the night before we flew to Tel Aviv. All I needed was a gun on my hip to join the security detail.

The peace skeptics at the first table scurried over to coo appreciatively for the Prime Minister. They recorded the unexpected meeting with their cell phones. As I reached for mine, Claudia ordered me to stop.

Once seated, Netanyahu engaged in a lively soliloquy his deep bass voice rolling under our table. When I turned around to sneak a peek he had both hands raised above his head much as mine were raised on the front page of the Duluth News Tribune two Decembers ago.

To say that Netanyahu is despised by peace types is putting it mildly. That didn't stop me from basking in the presence of power. I ordered coffee and desert to linger a little longer. And yet, over the next day I stewed about our close proximity. Claudia had shown me a galling story about Bibi in the Jerusalem Post before we saw him in the flesh. The story had stuck in my craw. The next day I wrote a pointed letter to the Post. It wasn't published.

Two weeks later, after our return to Duluth, the other bookend jumped out of my computer when I reviewed the thousands of pictures I had taken while in Israel. I'd shot one of them midway through our trip on a drive to the divided city of Hebron.

We had just left a Palestinian family in whose home we had stayed while near Bethlehem. They lived in Beit Sahour where the angels had directed shepherds to visit the manger. We pilgrims had enjoyed an energetic conversation at their breakfast table about war and peace before leaving. The family's daughter brought it to a close by mentioning that "someone is shot every day." That may have prompted me to take more pictures than usual of military checkpoints as we drove to the city where Abraham, Isaac and Jacob, lay buried under the Ibrahimi Mosque. Like Hebron the Mosque is divided into a Jewish and non Jewish half. No Jews have been admitted to the Muslim side since 1994. That was when an American Jew shot 29 worshipers dead while wounding another 125.

On one side of Hebron live ardent Jewish nationalists. They move into any home left vacant by Palestinians down on their luck on the Palestinian side of the city. Above the souk, or shopping district, wire mesh was strung to catch the garbage poured down on shoppers by Jewish squatters. To discourage mayhem IDF forces command Palestinian rooftops. We were all delighted by our Palestinian guide. We were to learn near the end of our trip that one of his legs was shorter from an Israeli soldier's bullet. He was full of mirth and good advice. He encouraged us not to buy goods from the many vendors who pursued us through every shopping district. But on this walk through Hebron he had only nice things to say about one such vendor. "He's a good guy." He told us. We found out later that the good guy, like our guide, had survived a gunshot during a protest.

At one of the last stalls we passed in the souk a merchant told our group resignedly that another Palestinian had been shot dead that day. We walked soberly under a canopy of trash back to our bus.

What we did not know, and what I would not learn until reviewing a fuzzy picture after my return to Duluth, was that our little band of peacemakers had driven right by that day's killing. Our bus driver had pulled into a road guarded by Israeli soldiers to turn around. As we paused I snapped a hasty picture of IDF trucks parked by razor wire. In the photo's lower right corner lay a dead man at the feet of an Israeli soldier. The body was stripped naked and sported angry red welts.

Harry Welty is a local eccentric and perennial candidate for office in Duluth who also pontificates on his blog: www.lincolndemocrat.com.

"HERE WERE HANGED"

Photo of and by Monroe P Killy circa 1930

"Here were hanged 38 Sioux Indians December 26 1862."

This was the Mankato "memorial" that greeted our family when we moved north from Topeka, Kansas in 1963. It was a five-ton, granite marker erected fifty years after the infamous deed and fifty years before my becoming a Minnesotan. I've never been clear about why it was erected. It was too terse to suggest either pride or remorse that Mankato had been the scene of America's largest mass hanging.

After it was erected it didn't take long for locals to complain that the "memorial" reflected badly on the pretty little town nestled in the Minnesota River Valley. Had they been consulted the few Dakota Indians left in southern Minnesota after the Great Sioux Uprising (Dakota War) would probably have objected too. Not only was it not a mea culpa, the word "Sioux" wasn't what the Dakota called themselves. "Sioux" came from the Ojibwe and reflected the centuries of conflict between their tribes. In Ojibwe "sioux" means snakelike whereas "Dakota," in Dakotan, means "friend."

The two-month uprising couldn't have come at a less opportune time for Minnesota. Many of its young European men were off fighting in the Civil War when the Dakota got tired of starving. The food promised them by treaty was not forthcoming. Consequently, angry young warriors, who couldn't help but notice that the whites were busy killing each other, decided to lend them a hand. It was a costly mistake. It only took two bloody months for the settlers and their army to route the Indians. 307 Dakota were sentenced to death until President Lincoln intervened and whittled the number down to 38. Thousands of vengeful white settlers attended the execution on the day after Christmas.

By the 1970s, after members of the American Indian Movement splashed red paint on the stone, the monument's days were numbered. The City eventually carted it off and buried it in a semi-secret location.

Every place I've lived has had its shameful episodes. That's what comes from having humans around. Shortly before Mankato's hanging, my birthplace, Kansas, was called "bleeding Kansas." Civic-minded fellows like Jesse James and John Brown were busy murdering each other lest the wrong side take control of the territorial legislature and adopt a pro-slavery or anti-slavery constitution.

A century after 1854's Bleeding Kansas came the 1954 Supreme Court decision, Brown vs. Topeka Board of Education. I vividly recall when the "colored school" in my neighborhood closed and its children were marched to my school.

Topeka's town fathers argued against integration. When the decision went against Topeka and the colored schools were closed it was the black teachers who lost their jobs.

How long should any people have to hang their heads over the misdeeds of their ancestors? Germans, have borne the shame and stigma of the Holocaust for fifty-five years even though 90 percent of the population was born after the war. I think Germany should be given credit for facing its history honestly. By contrast, Japan prefers to remember itself as a nuclear martyr for Hiroshima. The Japanese are still in denial about "comfort women," the "Rape of Nanking" and other war atrocities committed by their side. Few things are more seductive than a selective memory.

A few days ago I read a letter from a man who objected to the memorial Duluth plans to build for the lynchings of Elias Clayton, Elmer Jackson and Isaac McGhie. Its author didn't want to have to explain the memorial, or the stain on Duluth's history, to his grandchild.

There have been thousands of lynchings across the nation, from the civil war right up until my youth, but the 1920 Duluth lynching was notable. Black Americans realized that if a lynching could take place as far north as Duluth they weren't safe anywhere. This realization was so profound that a bright, young, black, college student at the University of Minnesota decided to dedicate his life to winning equal treatment for African Americans. Roy Wilkins became the chief legal strategist for the NAACP in the 1940's as that organization began to systematically challenge the Jim Crow laws, which hid behind the polite lie "separate but equal." Those challenges culminated in Brown v. Topeka Board of Education and that long line of black children who came to join me at Loman Hill Elementary when I was in second grade.

There is a new memorial in Mankato today next to the public library where 38 Sioux Indians were hung. It is a huge limestone Buffalo in what is now called "Reconciliation Park."

Reconciliation should be our aim too as we memorialize the murders of Clayton, Jackson and McGhie. It should not be regarded as an homage to infamy but rather as a testament to the path we've taken since. If we wish to stay on this new path we would do well to remember Santayana's warning. "Those who cannot remember the past are condemned to repeat it." This would be a worthy admonition for any grandfather to share with his grandchild.

Frybread Tacos
on the National Museum of the American Indian.
6th in a series on a visit to Washington DC
Nov. 23rd, 2023

Of all the Smithsonians in the Capital, none pulled more firmly on our party than the National Museum of the American Indian.

Constructed with Minnesota's Kasota stone quarried from the land where 38 Sioux Indians were hung on the Day after Christmas 1862, the curvilinear building looks like the wall of a southwestern canyon. Before their brutal exile, generations of Sioux walked over the stone as it filtered their sky-blue waters.

We walked to the museum along the National Mall on a hot day, taking cover under the shadows of spreading trees. After entering its lofty atrium, our first stop was the museum's lunchroom. It served Native American fare. We ordered frybread tacos with native toppings that would have satisfied a Super Bowl party.

The museum celebrates the diversity and future of our many native peoples. Overhead on every floor hang flags representing some 500 tribes, reservations and other divisions of people confined and/or removed from their lands for a greater good justified as being for their own good.

One of our grandsons traces back to the Chickasaw and Choctaw. Both tribes were force marched on trails of tears from the Deep South's rich black soils to enrich eastern bankers and land speculators intent on seizing their land. It would be planted in cotton and tended to by the labor of black slaves.

After starvation, cholera and hundreds of premature graves the "civilized tribes" were resettled in "Indian Territory." It was a dry and disappointing land but, they were assured, it would be theirs for all time.

The museum shows that despite years of movies with screaming feathered warriors circling wagon trains like ducks at a carnival shooting gallery, native peoples remain. Their languages stubbornly cling to old tongues. Their arts flourish. Their men and now women put their lives on the line for the defense of a nation that is still their home.

From the formation of reservations through my early childhood, native numbers flatlined, but that changed in the Civil Rights Era. In 1970 the Census reported a 66% increase in people with native ancestry while the nation's population only increased by 13 percent.

Only a people coming out of hiding could explain the jump from 551,000 to 827,000. From 1980 to 1990, native numbers more than doubled from 1,959,000 to 4,100,000 a 110 percent increase. By 2020, 9.7 million Americans claimed Indian ancestry. That was over 17 times more self-reported Native Americans in the last census than in 1960, not long before I moved to the depopulated Sioux lands of southern Minnesota.

Dozens of tribes were sent to Oklahoma with the promise of a forever land but America's leaders could not help themselves. Land rushes reopened "Indian territory" to new people eager to settle the last bit of frontier.

My great-grandfather McLatchey took his daughter's favorite horse to the Kansas/Oklahoma line to stake a claim for a new homestead at the sound of a starting gun. He damn near killed the horse only to find the claims were already staked by "Sooners," whose cheating ways became the beloved nickname for the people of the state. In time the takers forgot.

Famed Oklahoma cowboy-entertainer Will Rogers became America's favorite pre-war humorist. He joked, "I don't belong to any organized political party. I'm a Democrat." With a hint of native ancestry he helped the country forget broken promises. After the war another Rogers, composer Richard Rodgers, and his lyricist Oscar Hammerstein added more anesthesia in their sweeping Broadway musical Oklahoma where "the farmer and the cowman" could be friends. Oklahoma's farmers and cowmen did their best to share in the Osage's good fortune. The "Indian business," they called it.

The Osage, who had been given some of the least promising land, decided to protect what little they had by preventing individual Osage from selling any off. Every Osage owned a "head right." This was fortuitous because copious deposits of oil were discovered which made the Osage the richest people per capita in the world. In an Oklahoma that had just witnessed the aerial bombardment, looting and burning of Tulsa's "Black Wall-Street," this was especially prudent. To many it seemed a terrible shame that all this wealth was wasted on Indians.

But helpful outsiders could marry an Osage and many did. And then the Osage began dying mysteriously in the dozens and maybe the hundreds. Historian David Grann wrote a book about it – Killers of the Flower Moon. In the old days you wouldn't have seen this story on the big screen.

My grandfather had no use for Hollywood's treatment of history. Talked into seeing Errol Flynn play General Custer, he told his daughters afterward that Custer should have been court-martialed.

But today's Hollywood is Native America's friend. Director Martin Scorsese has turned the story into an epic three-and-a-half-hour movie of the same title. He's done this at a time when Oklahoma's Republican Legislators are trying to protect white children's feelings by stripping history out of their school books. As our children cut out pilgrims, Indians this Thanksgiving remember the Wampanoag Indians. They numbered perhaps 40,000 souls when the Pilgrims asked for their help. Today they number 3,200 while the descendants of the Pilgrims own Boston's Beacon Hill.

The federal government belatedly bestowed a reservation upon them in 2015. It's 150 Acres. The City of Duluth, by contrast, has 51,300 Acres.

Welty, a lucky full blooded "white" American can be ignored at lincolndemocrat.com.

NOTE: Both Mankato and Duluth have turned the page and have respectful memorials to their respective necktie parties. Topeka's old Monroe School is now a National Historical Park.

THE AMAZING COLOSSAL
DEFENDER OF DEMOCRACY
"It's OK to vote for Harry for the School Board"

The Amazing Colossal Defender of Democracy
Published March 21, 2024

I have a checkered history of promising to write books. You see in the image above one such example.

After tinkering with a poster for a 1950's B-movie I advertised my intention to write a book about the then recent Red Plan bulldozer that deprived Duluth voters of their right to vote on a half-billion-dollar plan to rebuild most of the City's public schools. In the process the District chased about 1,500 students out of the Duluth schools. It was an epic battle that consumed four years of my life. The fiasco was eminently worthy of the book I advertised. I collected sales from a 100 buyers before deciding its complexity exceeded my energy. I refunded all the sales.

I found the energy again on Jan. 6, 2021, when Donald Trump sent "patriots" to lynch Congress after he'd spent a year plotting to steal the 2020 election because polls predicted he would lose. If anything is sacred in a Democracy it's a fair election. America's elections only began being fair in 1965 when the Voting Rights Act stopped Dixiecrats (now called Republicans) from preventing black Americans from voting.

In recent years a "Republican" Supreme Court has used southern ideas like *"originalism"* and *"state's rights"* to give Republicans the power to tamper with fair elections. The starting gun for this sea-change began in 2000, when the Supreme Court found an exception to staying out of the state of Florida's business insuring that George W. Bush, the likely loser of the Florida presidential election, would be declared the winner. This was after Bush's win in the South Carolina Primary where his Dark Money supporters robo called every Republican voter to tell them that his opponent, John McCain, fathered a black child. That's another monstrosity the Republican Supreme Court has supercharged in **Citizens United v. the Federal Election Commission**. It allows the super rich to pour vast sums of money secretly into the campaign pockets of favored candidates under yet another innovative legal doctrine that says money is "free speech" protected by the First Amendment. Evidently rich have a lot more of it.

Throw in Donald Trump's discovery that a loser need not concede defeat, now being copied around the world by would be dictators, and you have the makings for Democracy's fall across the entire world.

Growing up I watched my Dad follow every nominating convention and stay up late for every election night's result. It impressed on me the importance of the elections America inspired all across the world. Here's a short anecdote that illustrates how deeply honest elections have become part of my DNA.

As a sophomore at Mankato State, I ran for reelection in the annual Student Senate race. Typically athletes and Greeks won the elections easily because only 1 in 10 students bothered to vote. The Fall election of 1970, became controversial when it was learned that Athletic Coaches had given lists of preferred candidates to their teams to vote for.

Non voting students didn't know what the coaches knew. The Student Senate exercised some serious influence on the spending of the Student Activity Fees paid by 15,000 students every quarter. The athletic teams got a piece of it. They wanted friends to help their cash-flow and I was a member of a fraternity they were collecting votes for.

One of my fraternity brothers was on the Wrestling team. He told me about the list he was given. I was outraged. How dare the teachers tamper with student votes!

Thinking about it now I don't see anything illegal about this. but it sure didn't smell right. I was probably more incensed than the independents who got outvoted. So I hustled over to confront the celebrated Rummy Macias.

I'd been to a couple wrestling meets and got a big kick out of Mrs. Macias who screamed support at every wrestler on Rummy's team until she was hoarse.

I demanded to know if it was true that Rummy had stuck his nose in the student's election. He was a tiny man and must have wrestled in the 100 pound weight class. He looked up at me bewildered that I, one of his beneficiaries, was raising hell. It probably didn't occur to me then that Rummy noticed my last name was the same as the president of the Faculty union. He stammered a bit and that was enough for me so I left. I'd made my point. Then I supported the outcome of the election because the lucky winners hadn't done anything wrong and it would have been a hassle to re-vote. Its nice when pragmatism helps your side out. It strikes me that this kind of reasoning may be even more persuasive to the Republican Supreme Court than its Dixiecrat judicial doctrines.

The next year, 1972, a constitutional amendment went into effect allowing 18-year-olds to vote for the first time. The Nixon-supporting Republicans were worried sick that students would cast anti-Vietnam votes against them everywhere. By 1972 I'd become a Republican and I dipped into my pocket to use my free speech rights to convince students to vote for a Republican State Senator. He hadn't bothered to campaign on the campus with its 12,000 new voters. My hand out got him elected. The banker he defeated was not happy. The loser's college supporters told me their man gave some thought to suing me. But that's a story for Volume 2. If I write it.

And what of the section subtitle about its being OK to vote for me for the School Board? That was the word from a fellow Republican to her friends. It was OK to vote for me because my being on the school board, unlike the Legislature, meant I couldn't vote for pro-choice laws even if I was a baby killer.

And some thoughts about sociopaths...

Not your usual Republican
Published March 28, 2024

This is Volume 1.
Will there be a Volume II?

My wife, Claudia, pointed out the obvious to me. My soon-to-be-published book's front cover has a lie on it. She kindly called it an exaggeration. I was delighted. She reads circles around me - two or three books a week since we were married just short of fifty years ago. Just how much is 2 x 52 weeks x 50 years? Holy cow!

Until I handed her 300 pages pulled mostly from my Reader columns she rarely if ever read them. She's watched me hide in my office for hours over the last six years laboring to sew a Frankenstein monster of a book together out of them. She suggested they weren't half bad.

Her skirting my work began 22 years ago, when I read her my take down of a wannabe Rush Limbaugh who called me ACDC on his radio program. I didn't like being called "politically bisexual." I have a turn the other cheek policy.....Once. But like Michelle Obama, Claudia is more of a "when they go low we go high" kind of person.

Wary of my reputation, she told me I was never to write about her, *especially* her work. She was furious when her workmates deduced that she might retire, when I wrote that she was planning to study at a seminary after retiring. I was proud of her and couldn't help myself. My columns have been mini 800-word autobiographies from the beginning. Authors are always encouraged to write what they know. I know me.

I do use the words "I' and "my" a lot. In commemorating the life of Bob Mars a few years ago I mentioned that Bob told me I used the word "I" too much. Other Board members often complained to him when I wrote about what the school board was up to and why. Its very true. When I look at the world I write about, I can't help but use the I word. And that sentence is a perfect example. It's got four I's.

For some inexplicable reason **Not Your Usual Republican** and its predecessor **Not Eudora** always took my side. I did take a lot of vacations from the NOTS. I did it when my name was on the ballot. I've been on the ballot eleven times since "Monkeyworms" was published in 2002. I switched to writing in my blog during the war over the Red Plan. I needed to send out information daily to my allies about the sociopath leading the Duluth Schools. Sociopath is a clinical word for someone who can lie without pangs of conscience. I think about one in 14 people qualify which is fewer than the 1 in 10 who are believed to be gay.

I think sociopaths are easier to catch in grade school while they are still testing the waters to see how much they can get away with. They soon learn to use their special power sparingly only when they are unlikely to be caught. Having everyone call you a liar is bad for business. It's a talent and evolution favors useful traits. A nation needs spies who can lie convincingly. Many police and corporate execs are said to be sociopaths. Your neighbor might be one. You might be too.

I didn't catch on at first. I was one of the new Superintendents supporters until some things didn't add up. I eventually found a video of him on his first day at work in Duluth. Keith Dixon talked on film about race his first day and described his black college friend who told him all about his travails as a black kid. Two years later I called the kid up. He was a retired Minnesota Viking. He told me he'd never talked to Dixon in college. Despite that Keith damn near came to tears on tape describing the heart rending story he'd heard about racism from his acquaintance.

During the hashtag "me too" movement, long after Dixon won the Red Plan fight, I was sent an email inquiry by a woman who told me Dixon, a school administrator, had threatened her in high school. Curious about what had happened to the man she had babysat for she'd googled Dixon's name and found all my blog posts calling him a "liar."

Like Dixon, most sociopaths are pretty covert. But today we have a billionaire sociopath trying to get back into the Oval Office and his supporters like his lying even more than evolution does. What's Donald Trump's appeal? His supporters think his lies are telling it like it is. They know he's lying but he's doing it to taunt their enemies in the Deep State, liberal *bureaucrats*, or the liberal media that looks down on them. Trump's supporters want the good ole days back.

I have a different notion of the good ole days. Mike Jaros who admits to reading my column is a part of my good ole days. He cleaned my clock in two campaigns for the state legislature. When I came to Duluth in 1974 I was hoping to run for political office. After a desperately weak, candidate hungry,

Republican Party nominated me I called Mike to introduce myself as his new challenger. We had coffee at Perkins and enjoyed a cordial conversation. Mike bunked in a hotel with another democrat and legislator that I had campaigned for in Mankato. He was a neighbor and. I wasn't sorry to see the republican incumbent who was suffering from Alzheimers lose to him. To be clear this fellow was running for the House. The same year, 1972, I got a Republican elected the State Senate.

Mike was also a friend of my geography teacher who had a thicker Yugoslavian accent than Jaros. Mike misses Republicans like me. He misses Republicans who compromised and made the legislature work even if they called Mike an ultra socialist.

Oh yeah, about that lie on the front cover of my book. I claim to have predicted Trump would take over the Republican Party in 1992. The truth is, his was just one of a half dozen sleazy businessmen I listed telling the delegates they were the kind of people who would be running the party. That's close enough for me.

Welty can't wait to hobnob with Marjorie Taylor Greene and Matt Gaetz in DC to see if they wet their pants. Stay tuned at www.lincolndemocrat.com

THE SOUTH'S SCARLET LETTER

The hurt the South won't forget and The resentment it has spread across America

In the decades leading up to the Civil War the slave south hated one word above all others. "ABOLITION." It was an accusation that the South was ungodly. When White Southerners took over again following "Reconstruction" they resumed practices that were a stain on the Declaration of Independence. The echoes of that stain can be heard wherever "wokeness" is decried today and history textbooks are bleached white by indignant legislators spreading sleeping sickness.

While I attended an integrated school and Civil Rights pressed ahead, the white South fought to protect their white children from this calamity. To a remarkable degree they succeeded. As their old allies in the big northern cities abandoned them the crafty South made common cause with the once despised "Papists." In the age of "the pill," virgin venerating Rome hated fornication above all other sins. Contraception made sex too tempting. So too Abortion. These convictions were joined to the doctrine that souls were created at conception.

These doctrines were unfamiliar to the southern Church. For plantation owners sex was simply the siring of property that could be sold to help the bottom line. Southern churches had fairly straight forward remedies for unconstrained sex. It was lynchings for interracial couples if the man was black; shotgun weddings when it was an all-white affair.

This pragmatic South understood that allying themselves with Catholics could help them hold onto congressional majorities. When they figured out that six-month-old babies were more adorable than gnarly fetuses on Highway billboards they took off. Now the South had a scarlet letter to throw back at the smug self righteous North. ABORTION!

I did not expect the famously randy Donald Trump to become President in 1992 when I gave the following speech. However, I suspected where equating abortion with baby killing would take politicians who hated paying taxes for unwanted children.

My 1992 Speech at the Radisson Hotel (as originally delivered)

The first time I addressed a Republican convention was right here in this very hallway. That was twenty years ago last April. It was not my finest hour. I was campaigning to be the President of the Minnesota State College Republicans. My only rival did not want the job. He left the Convention without even addressing the delegates to ask for their vote. It might just as well have been an uncontested election. I was certain of victory. As I addressed the convention my rival was already in his car heading home. - I lost.

When I got up to speak I was seized by such a violent attack of nerves that I astonished the expectant delegates. I gibbered for five nervous minutes. It was an out of body experience for me. My spirit slipped away from me, and hovered overhead watching my body blather incoherently. Today I plan to set that failure to rights. There will be no ad-libbing this time. I've typed out my speech and my spirit is very much inside my body. Its too bad the results will be the same as they were twenty years ago.

Ladies and Gentlemen of the Grand Old Party: I am troubled about the unsteady course America is steering. Our children are about to inherit problems as great or greater than those we faced in our childhood. Unfortunately, our children will not have the advantage of an unrivaled America with unparalleled resources. Instead our children will inherit a crippled, debtor, nation with a large population of economically marginal citizens. We can not allow this to continue. It is time for us to sacrifice for our children. We must stop making our children sacrifice for us.

I speak from personal experience. Let me explain: Most of you are aware of the difficulties that have bedeviled the Duluth Schools. Several years have passed and problems which were once merely monumental have become intractable. My children will survive these difficulties just as sheltered, upper, middle-class children have for generations. I wish I could say the same for less fortunate children.

Last year when I ran for the school Board, I discovered a dirty little secret. I discovered that twenty percent of Duluth's children drop out of school. If you walk into one of our elementary classrooms, look hard. One in five of the children you see, will not graduate. This is a public relations nightmare for our School Administration which insists that we have a mere six percent dropout rate. But this claim is purely self delusion. It is a delusion which is self destructive. It is a delusion that is symbolic of an America we would rather not acknowledge. We are a nation wearing blinders. Ignorance, is our narcotic, and it is a powerful narcotic.

Let me tell you about my children's elementary school. In rainy weather, the custodians set out dozens of trash cans to collect the water which seeps through a sodden roof. No matter. Our city has twice turned down school bonds in recent years. Ironically, my children's elementary school wasn't even included in the bonds because it is one of the better buildings.

This is Duluth. A city which will not voluntarily raise money to repair the roofs of its schools, but just seven blocks from my house is a federal project which cost One-Quarter-of-a-Billion-Dollars, seven times as much as the most recent school bond. This federal project is a vast concrete tunnel carved into Duluth's hard, basaltic, rock for an interstate highway which, when it is completed, will save me two minutes when I drive down town.

A nation that gives precedence to two minutes of my life over the future of my child has it priorities tragically backwards. Who do I blame? I blame myself. I blame you. I blame all of us for electing representatives, like our Congressman James Oberstar, who are responsible for our vast, misdirected, national budget. Its our fault that we haven't sent our Congress a clear, unselfish message. It has been half a century since there was a serious general election campaign for Congress in Minnesota's Eighth Congressional District. That was 1946! We must not wait any longer. Ladies and gentleman. This is the Twentieth Century! Its time for us to follow Russia's example, and have real democratic elections in northern Minnesota. This Congress must be challenged. Congressman Oberstar must be challenged. We can not - We must not - allow our Congress to impoverish our children for our temporary convenience.

My fellow Republicans, I regret to tell you, that your candidate, Phil Herwig, is not the man to challenge Congressman Oberstar. Even though he will certainly win your endorsement, I will do my best to be the Party's candidate in November by winning the September primary. Sadly, I suspect that if I win the primary, many of you will quietly vote for Jim Oberstar. If you do vote for Jim Oberstar I will understand. You have no choice. Jim Oberstar is Pro-life and I am pro-choice.

I have not come here in anger. Unlike many pro-choice partisans I have a deep respect for the motives which have impelled you to join and take over the Republican party.

I don't keep track of aborted babies but I know there have been millions since Roe vs. Wade. I know you would prefer to blame these callous, medical, procedures on those of us who are stubbornly pro-choice. Certainly, no one can accuse the pro-life lobby of sitting back idly over the past twenty years. But if you truly want to end what you regard as a slaughter of innocents, I urge you to ask yourselves these questions. Why, have you failed so utterly to stem the tide of abortion? Why, have you failed to rally a clear majority of the electorate to your cause? Why, have so many of your formerly stalwart pro-life representatives, like Congressman Sikorski, jumped ship as Roe v Wade slips into the judicial sunset.

Take a minute to look beyond the imminent Supreme Court reversal of Roe. What will happen then? Will abortions end? No! They will not! What will you do when you discover that Roe's reversal is only a pyrrhic victory? What will you do when abortions continue largely unabated. The war between our respective sides will continue state by state, and in the Congress, but abortions will continue.

I am pro-choice. I will go further; I am fiercely pro-choice. I have been pro-choice for a quarter of a century, ever since I was a virginal, high school Junior. Ironically, I too want to see an end to abortion as a method of birth control. Listen to me. It is only in alliance with people like me that abortion will ever be ended in this nation. You will not legislate it out of existence.

Let me leave you with this bitter observation. The Republican party has become a party which revels in its criticism of Welfare Queens and become a party which tolerates, even worships, the Donald Trumps, Michael Milkins, Charles Keatings and Ivan Boeskies of the world.

We are a political party which abhors the redistribution of wealth and yet, in the last twelve years America's rich have gotten richer while America's poor have gotten poorer. There has been such disintegration of society that one American child in 5 lives in poverty. There are more abortions in this nation than you realize, because for many children life is an abortion. These children are, homeless; neglected; ill educated; prone to prostitution, AIDS, crack cocaine, guns, violent deaths, joblessness, and hopelessness. These children live lives that are a prolonged bath of scalding salt.

How can the party of Lincoln ever hope to end abortion, or win the public's sympathy, when it turns its back on the very children it is determined to see born?

THE CRIMES OF
BARACK OBAMA

     I've clipped out political cartoons over the years and pinned them to my bulletin board. One of my favorites by editorial cartoonist Oliphant shows an eager College Republican cheering for Richard Nixon in 1972 with a worldly Vietnam Vet wearily looking on. It's next to Peanut's Snoopy hailing Willie and Joe on Veterans Day. Willie and Joe were the famous GI dogfaces that Bill Maudlin drew slogging along in World War II. I also have a 2008 cartoon with the statue of Lincoln in his D.C. memorial giving a small silhouette of Barack Obama a thumbs up. This was during my short stay in the Democratic party. Obama's election was the most gratifying event of my political life. Not everybody was so thrilled. I heard a white guy tells an NPR reporter matter-of-factly "I voted for the n-------." Talk about a sour thumbs up.

The Crimes of Barack Obama
Published Apri 23, 2020

The passing of the torch and the pressing of the flesh at the transition of the Presidency in 2017

It was necessary to elect Donald Trump because of the crimes of Barack Obama. I probably won't remember them all any more than I can remember a day's worth of President Trump's crimes. I'll start with the first which is clear to me because I thought about it a great deal as an elementary school kid. That was in the Sixties during the centennial of the Civil War. My Topeka, Kansas, elementary school had just been integrated making me one of the few white kids in America who ever actually sat side-by-side with more than one or two black kids in class. Wondering when a "Negro" might actually have chance to get elected President I did a little mental math.

At the time there were still about ten states that made it impossible for blacks to vote. They also had laws against letting black and white people marry. It had taken a hundred years to integrate schools so I figured it would take another hundred for there to be a black President. I was off by 50 years.

Instead of 2060 Barack Obama got elected in 2012. That was Obama's first crime. It was only possible because the hapless Bush Administration resumed a war with Iraq, sat on its thumb while New Orleans was laid waste followed by the Republican's deregulated home mortgage rules causing the loss of millions of homes and bringing the world to a hair's breadth from a second Depression.

Ironically, Obama's election was abetted by

"conservative" screamers like Rush Limbaugh who thought the real menace was a woman, Hillary Clinton. Rush and his mini-me's told their listeners that Obama was a much more gifted candidate than the former first lady. (Shades of their praise for Bernie Sanders?) But what they were counting on was another Thomas Bradley to guarantee a Republican victory. When black Los Angeles Mayor, Bradley, ran to be Governor of California the polls all said he was a shoe-in - except that the voters lied to the pollsters. Afraid that they might be considered racists many voters didn't tell pollsters the truth. So, Limbaugh and his minions, hoping for a repeat, heaped praise on Obama because he was sure to lose like Mayor Bradley.

I had more faith in American voters. I thought Americans were tired of living in a racist America. Sure enough, Rush Limbaugh's calculations blew up in his face. That was Barack Obama's first crime. Getting elected fifty years too soon.

Black kids learn early from their parents to be squeaky clean and Obama was no exception. He led the least corrupt Administration in U.S. History. But Limbaughers weren't all wrong about white concerns. They argued that Civil Rights was no longer needed. Then they sniffed that Obama was arrogant for saying that "elections have consequences..." And then Obama committed Crime number two. He had the gall to enact what he had campaigned for.

Obama wanted to expand America's stingy medical coverage to people who depended on emergency rooms. GOP Senator Mitch McConnell, intent on keeping America the stingiest nation in the Free World told the press that his priority was ensuring that Obama became a one-term president. Health care would require every Democratic Senator to support Obama's plan even if they represented "red" states. Obama passed the Affordable Care Act without a single Republican vote.

The President's third crime was telling a lie to pass the Affordable Care Act. The new law did not guarantee Americans the right to use the doctors of their choice. Sensing that fudging this was the only way to cover tens of millions of uninsured Americans, Obama made the guarantee. It's one lie vs. 12,000 for Obama's successor but it cost the Democratic Senators who voted to insure America. After he won control of the Senate Mitch McConnell would get six years to show the consequence of winning elections.

Obama's fourth crime would be repeated every time a cop killed an unarmed black citizen. The President sympathized with the victims. The first offense didn't involve a killing. It was a simple arrest of a black professor for walking into his own house in Boston. Henry Louis Gates, who you may recognize from the PBS show on genealogy, was reported to police by a neighbor who thought it was suspicious that a black man would walk into a house in her neighborhood.

After Professor Gate's arrest Obama said something unpardonable. He said it was obvious that the cop had acted in haste. How dare he? Limbaugh had assured white people that civil rights was over now and here was a black president sticking up for black people. When President Obama tried to sooth White America's hurt feelings by inviting the cop and the professor to a "beer summit" in the Rose Garden the Fox News Crowd sneered.

Every time a black kid was shot and the President cried foul Republicans were outraged. When school children of any race were shot en masse their voter's first concern was that Obama was going to take guns away. After his reelection fearful gun worshipers stormed gun stores to stock up on guns the way corona-virus worriers had fistfights over toilet paper. Assaulting the Second Amendment was Obama's fifth crime.

Finally, when a blowhard TV billionaire jetted around the country claiming that Barack Obama was a Kenyan only to have the State of Hawaii provide the President's birth certificate Obama was provoked into committing his sixth crime. He roasted Donald Trump at the White House Correspondents Dinner. Imagine that! A president treating real news as fake!!! Only a fake president would do that.

Welty takes more potshots at Trump at:lincolndemocrat.com

WE ARE THE METEOR

Published Nov. 10, 2022

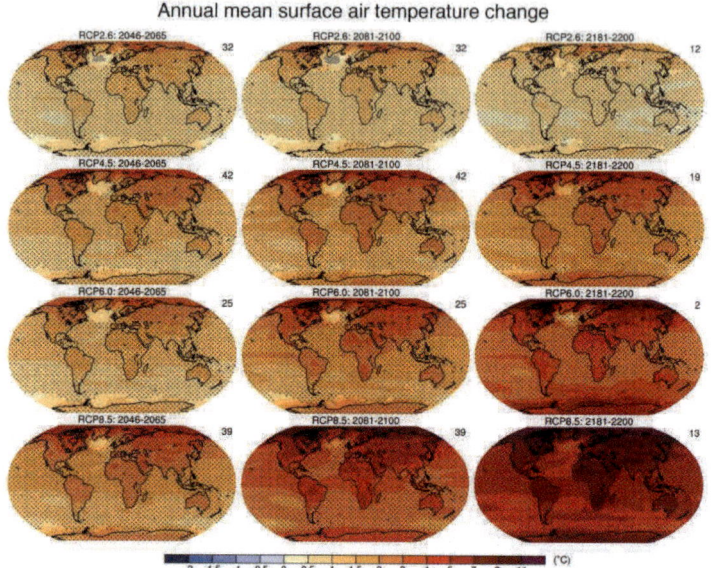

Annual mean surface air temperature change

If you were to put the phrase "my buddy" in the search box of my blog you would find over two hundreds posts about my political fencing with Vic, now deceased. Until his death I always referred to him as "My Buddy." He was a city attorney whose eccentricities probably cost him his job. I suspected he was on "the spectrum."

We spent twenty years chewing over politics in emails. He never once acknowledged having misspoken or amended his judgments. Damned attorneys! My wife who worked in the City's Personnel Office got to know him while the FBI was investigating local Democrats. I was a budding Republican who was cheeky enough to send a fundraising letter to her boss, one of Duluth's most cold blooded Democrats.

Vic swore he was an independent but over time he grew increasingly critical of many of my Republican heresies. He was particularly annoyed with my conviction that police leaned too heavily on black Americans. He tattled on me by sending one of my blog posts to that affect to Duluth's Chief of Police. The Chief emailed back that Vic, ought "to consider the source." By the time you are reading this we will know if the old chief has become our new St. Louis County Sheriff.

In about 2009 Vic and I dug our heels in opposite directions over "Climategate." With far less evidence than exists today I worried about the fate of the Earth. It had been a Republican cause as far back as Teddy Roosevelt. In the 1980's Republican President George H.W. Bush pushed for carbon offsets a small step in the right direction. But with the introduction of the human torch Newt Gingrich in the 90's and the Koch Brother's plying the GOP with dark money "climate denialism" took its place as the party's new 11th commandment.

A secret network of well financed Koch climate deniers began pulling CIA level stunts to cast doubt on climate change. They got hold of emails exchanged between frustrated scientists who were shocked by political indifference to their evidence of a looming climate catastrophe. Their emails were made public and they were roundly accused of only being interested in keeping government funding flowing into their paychecks. It was forgotten that big oil, gas and coal had a significant pecuniary interest in downplaying disaster. Sending more CO_2 into the sky and ocean meant billions to their investors. Their billions helped finance dark money donations to political collaborators who helped them keep on polluting. Until the last couple years of growing environmental horrors the denialists had the upper hand. Climate fixers lost a precious decade. My Buddy was on Darth Vader's side.

To me, the emails were simply shop talk. To Vic they were proof of hysteria. He told me he was more worried about a meteor hitting Earth. I much prefer the odds of facing a killer asteroid to CO_2 burning climate change. The dinosaurs got 200 million uninterrupted years. Mammals have only had 65 million so far. I'm pretty sure we can bank on a good thousand years free and clear from space. Just last week scientists, silly, silly scientists, nudged a solar spit ball out of its orbit. Its not a meteor that is causing the "sixth extinction." Its us.

There is an insect apocalypse and a bird apocalypse playing out today. Blue whales are eating 96 pounds of micro plastics each day. The liberal New York times and Washington Post cover these calamities every day not horse blinder wearing Fox News. The buried carbon from hundreds of millions of years of dead trees has been released by modern man into our atmosphere in mere centuries. Above our heads a trillion tons of it floats. Its the weight of every structure ever built by humans. We are babies in a car's back seat on a hot day.

But you can't see a trillion tons in invisible air. You can't see plastic micro pellets in the ocean. You can't see the forever chemicals which turn male frogs into females. If you can't see it how can you trust science when anonymous trolls on Facebook, Google and Twitter confidently lie that its not so.

It's ironic that the Republican party is the party of abortion. They are aborting the Earth. Once they have accomplished this all the little fetuses they worship, before becoming inconvenient humans, will face a future rather like the 150 Korean kids last Halloween night. They were trampled to death in Seoul's too narrow streets as some of them cried "Push" like a CO_2 lobbyist.

So Vic you were smug, eccentric and wrong. You could afford to be. You never had kids. I wish being an "I told you so" gave me some comfort but I'm only left with a great sorrow that the apology I owe my grandchildren is worth no more than the ink in my laser printer. We are the Meteor, Vic. We are the Earth's abortionist.

Welty also shoots his mouth off at:lincolndemocrat.com

AND JUST FOR FUN

The Furries are coming for us

Thursday May. 26th, 2022

In 1992, after giving a speech at a congressional district endorsing convention and drawing boos from most of the Republican delegates, I got a lecture. A solid Duluth businessman told me that challenging the endorsed candidate was wrong and that he couldn't support me.

Cut to the 2022 convention where I was unable to give a speech. This gentleman's son, now in charge of his father's business, engaged me in a friendly conversation.

Knowing what made me the wrong kind of Republican, he set me straight about the world we lived in. He had been talking with business people all over the upper Midwest who, like him, worked with public schools. They had all been sharing the shocking news that their school boards were welcoming a perverse political correctness into the classroom. Children identifying as animals were demanding to be treated like cats and dogs in class and the schools were going along with it. Teachers were being forced to conduct class with children dressed as cats sitting at their feet. Kitty litter boxes were being put in school bathrooms.

Given the businessman's many eyewitnesses, I listened politely if skeptically. I had been substitute teaching in a school that looked kindly on odd duck kids. I had seen some girls who drew hearts on their noses and who teased their hair to suggest a feline look. However, none of them ever purred or meowed at me.

Did all these businessmen sharing this nonsense and eager to believe it really represent today's Republican Party?

It's not a first. Abraham Lincoln famously joked about the Millerites of his era. Mr. Miller, a Revelations reading doomsday-er, convinced thousands of Americans to sell their farms to prepare for the end of days. When his first prediction of apocalypse fell through he recalculated the Bible's hints. His hopeful End-timers prepared anew for the appointed apocalypse. When instead another day dawned the Millerites mostly, but never completely, died out.

The one-time Republican Presidential candidate, the Reverend Pat Robertson, recently explained that God is directing Putin's invasion of the Ukraine. Better sell your farms!

The End of times has been predicted again and again. The entire last thousand years was a big mistake. We were supposed to come to an end in the year 1,000. The too-eager Millerites only jumped the gun 150 years prematurely. The new counting system made the year 2000 the new 1000. The Bible never lies. God just has tricky math.

As the year 2000 approached good Christian Republicans were primed for the "rapture." They knew they would be lifted to heaven leaving piles of clothes behind for the damned "Left Behind" to envy.

At Minnesota Power my wife was one of the people tasked with making sure the computers did not all shut down at the stroke of 2000, thus ending the generation of electricity while airplanes fell from the sky. Both catastrophes were avoided.

Today rapture fever depends on whether Republicans can persuade America that an arrogant used car salesman won a majority of the votes after letting a million citizens die of the virus he bungled.

Maybe God is in on the "big lie" too. After all, an America that will fall for the story that schools are putting cat litter boxes in their rest rooms is sure to snap up Fox News's "Replacement Theory." Move over "Chronicles of the Elders of Zion."

Now we know that crafty Jews recruited stoopid black people to board slave ships to replace white people. And that was only their second sneaky replacement. The first time they recruited stoopid white people to replace America's red people.

Republicans are allergic to the scientific version of end times. Until they leave their piles of cloths behind, they want to keep enjoying cheap hamburgers and leather car seats while suffocating God's green Earth and dooming billions of species Noah once rescued to oblivion.

I would dearly love to be like Abe Lincoln and find gentle humor in superstitious white voter's anxieties. But poor Abe. When he called for malice toward none, white supremacist extraordinaire, John Wilkes Booth, shot him in the back of the head.

That's Congressman Pete Stauber's Republican Party today. Twice he's sworn this oath of office:

"I, Pete Stauber, do solemnly swear (or affirm) that I will support and defend the Constitution of the United States against all enemies, foreign and domestic; that I will bear true faith and allegiance to the same; that I take this obligation freely, without any mental reservation or purpose of evasion, and that I will well and faithfully discharge the duties of the office on which I am about to enter. So help me God."

With Pete in Congress we are safe from the Furries.

Everything Harry writes that is not about the imminent destruction of Earth as we knew it is superfluous. But, he does prattle on at lincolndemocrat.com.

Welcome to College Andrew

Sept. 11, 2008, Duluth Reader.

ANOTHER SHOT   2-22-96

CHARLES CURTIS/NEWS-TRIBUNE

It's ready and this time it's the University of Minnesota-Duluth Bulldog wielding a hockey stick. Harry Welty has continued his annual tradition of creating a giant snow sculpture in his front yard at 21st Avenue East and Fourth Street. Welty has taken some kidding from Duluthians who found him remiss in his annual snow-sculpting duty after he was elected to the School Board last fall.

Labor Day has become the day my wife most wants to leave town. It's not the cause that vexes her. It's the spring-like smelt run of college students back to the North Shore. This year we were unable to make our egress.

The beer parties along 21st Ave. East were out in full force Friday evening. The kids across the street were passing out beer in red plastic cups and playing been bag much as my generation would have played foosball only out on the front lawn. We didn't rush to the windows when five police cruisers charged up the avenue lights blazing, sirens blaring. We were however, grateful to read later of the 71 visits they made to neighborhood parties to damper them.

I missed the hubbub as gaggles of kids drifted between parties because I hid in my basement painting till midnight . Claudia babysat our year-old grandson upstairs and channeled her attention to him. They were both asleep by the time I crawled under the covers and I was soon in the welcoming arms of Morpheus and dead to the world.

The sheets were tugged off my shoulder. "Where is everybody?" asked the sheet-tugger in his low voice. I rolled over toward the door and blinked up from my pillow at a young man who looked at me as he leaned carelessly against the door jamb. "Where is everybody?" he asked again right at home. The light from the room across the hallway lit him up in the darkness. I had turned that light out.

My brain switched focus from: "Darn, I wanted to finish that dream." to "Unnhh," to "Who's the kid who pulled off my sheets?"

"This kid is drunk on his ass," my brain helpfully explained.

"Where is everybody?" the kid asked again.

"You're in the wrong house." My mouth replied.

"No, I'm not," the drunk boy said.

"Yes you are." I insisted, "and you're drunk and I went to bed stone cold sober." The drunk boy just stared down at me.

"Do you know where you are supposed to be?" I asked him by now aware that I was alone in the bed. I could guess that Grandma had left our queen earlier to watch over our grandson. Since she often wakes to nightmares with a scream this was a blessing.

This was not the first college student to stumble into our home when I'd forgotten to lock the back door. A few years back I found one sleeping on the couch in our basement and assumed he was my son's friend. When he awoke the next morning he climbed the stairs, walked outside, turned around and blinked a couple times at the door trying to figure out where he was and how he'd got there.

Another drunken kid walked into my back yard one winter night and stood staring at my back door for five minutes.

I spent an hour driving him around trying to figure out where he was supposed to be. He finally gave me the phone number of his girl friend back home in the Twin Cities.

Her father answered the phone at three in the morning. I explained my predicament to him and he called his daughter to the phone to help me out. I've always wondered how that relationship fared after that call.

This night I pulled some pants on and led my sodden guest down the stairs and looked out the front door hoping that the party across the street was still in full swing. All that was left there was a table with two dozen red cups standing on it waiting for the party's resumption. All was quiet the parties and the cops having left the field of combat.

My uninvited guest plunged past me down the stairway with me trailing reluctantly behind. I was barefoot. I asked him what his name was and where he was from. He was Andrew from Cloquet.

He crossed the avenue and headed uphill looking back at me to make sure I was following. I thought about my bare feet. I thought about broken shards of beer bottle. I thought about its being 3AM. I thought about trying to corral a bull headed kid who didn't know where he was going. I thought about my bed and the dream I wanted to finish. I thought about how guilty I would feel the following morning if I heard that a college kid had been hit by a car. Not guilty enough I decided. I left Andrew to his own devices and headed home.

My wife and grandson were in the kitchen warming up a bottle. My wife had no idea that our Grandson had woken up because of the conversation he had overheard. She thought the radio alarm had gone off.

Welcome to Duluth Andrew. I hope you made it back safe to wherever you were headed.

Welty is a small time politician who lets it all hang out at: www.letduluthvote.com

You can help Harry financially in two ways.

1st You can buy his, *this*, book. If you want a hard copy order it on www.weltyforcongress.com, Harry's campaign website. It will cost roughly $25 plus mailing. Or, you can buy it for your Kindle at between $5 to $10. After Amazon's cut Harry is free to spend any earnings, *Harry's earnings*, on his campaign.

2nd If you would like to donate to **weltyforcongress**.com go to the page that looks like the one below. Push the donation button.

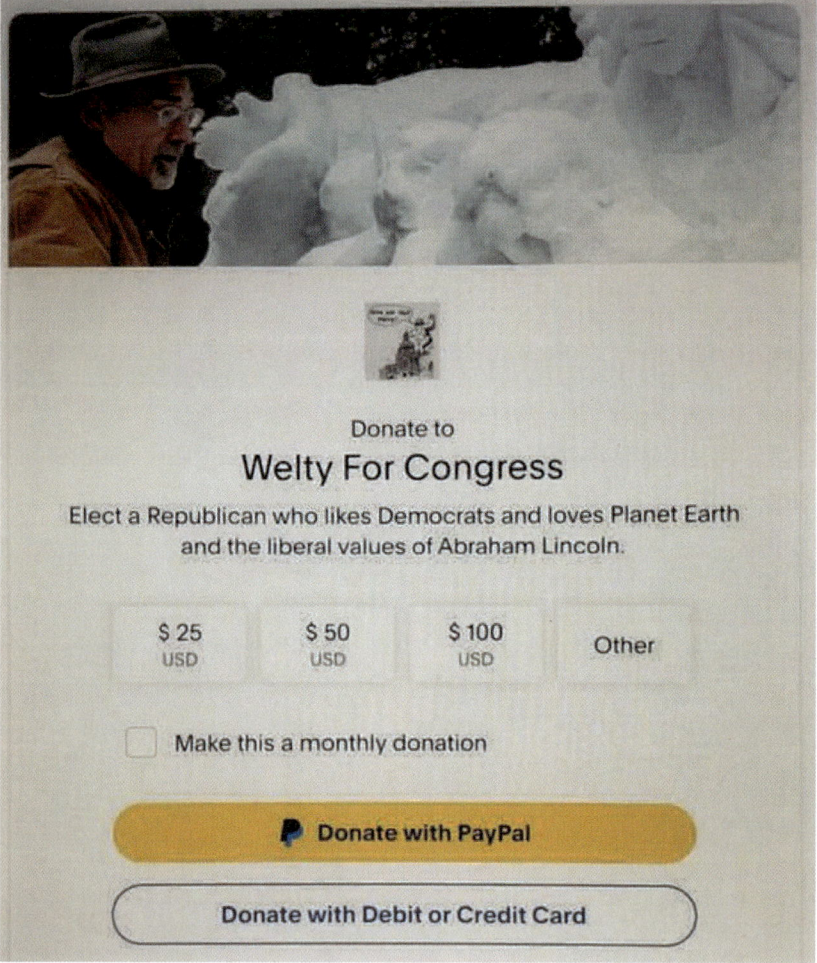

If you've forgotten why its important look a the back page of the book.